and

the Jesuits

BY
THEODORE
MAYNARD

P. J. KENEDY & SONS
New York

NIHIL OBSTAT:
    Carolus E. Diviney
        Censor Librorum
IMPRIMATUR:
    ✠ Thomas Edmundus Molloy, S.T.D.
        Archiepiscopus-Episcopus Brooklyniensis
Brooklynii
    Die XVI Februarii, 1956

SAINT IGNATIUS
and THE JESUITS

Saint Ignatius

In Memoriam

J. J. D., S.J.
F. X. T., S.J.
T. D., S.J.

Contents

Acknowledgments

MY THANKS should be given to a number of people for the loan of books, especially to Father Joseph D. Ryan, S.J., who seems to be constantly commuting between Inisfada, the Jesuit house at Manhasset, Long Island, and the new Bellarmine College at Plattsburg, N.Y., of which he is the librarian; the Very Reverend Matthew Hoehn, O.S.B., of St. Mary's Abbey, Newark, N.J.; Miss Helen B. Curtice and Miss Catherine Sandy of the Public Library of Port Washington, New York, through whom books were secured at the State Library at Albany, N.Y.; and Mr. Joseph T. Hart, the librarian of Fordham University.

In addition I must thank the Reverend E. A. Ryan of Woodstock College and the Reverend Martin P. Harney of Boston College for reading my book in manuscript and for the many valuable suggestions they have made.

Introduction

It is probable that around no group of men have so many misconceptions grown up as around the members of the Society founded by Ignatius of Loyola. To clear the road I would like to deal with certain of these right at the start and especially with the matters of the Jesuits' so-called military character and the nature of their vow of obedience.

A military order in the ordinary historical sense the Jesuits certainly never were, nor have there been any such founded since the time of the Crusades. The first of them, the Templars, came into being early in the twelfth century for the defense of the Kingdom of Jerusalem, but eventually grew so wealthy and corrupt—though most of the charges brought against them were not well founded—that about two hundred years later they were suppressed in France by the Holy See, as they were a little later in England and Spain. Most of the old military orders are long since extinct or have become purely secular orders of knighthood. Among those that have retained some features of their ecclesiastical character are the Knights of Malta, the Teutonic Order, the Order of the Holy Sepulchre, and certain Spanish military orders, but these are mainly decorative affairs. Obviously the Jesuits never had any resemblance to organizations of this sort. If they are to be styled "military," it must be in the completely different sense of those engaged, under the standard of Christ, in the struggles for victories that are spiritual.

1

Nor has their term "General" any military connotation, for many of the religious orders founded since the thirteenth century have the same title for the man in that position. Neither should it be forgotten that centralization in religious life had often occurred before Ignatius' day. Even some Benedictine groups gave up their characteristic autonomy in order to put themselves under the direction of one who was in effect a general, as in the case of the numerous Cluniac dependencies which made themselves subject to the abbot of the main monastery. Later the Franciscans and Dominicans, upon finding that mobility was essential to their work, also found that they needed a general to be in charge.

In this respect the Jesuits introduced no new principle. Their novelty was the abolishing of the capitular system. The medieval orders had their provincials and, in some cases, their rectors or priors. In the Society of Jesus, the General is, it is true, elected by electors who are in turn elected — the appointed provincials among them being *ex officio* — but all other offices are at the disposition of the General, and he holds office for life.

This much may be said; the organization of the Society of Jesus is minutely outlined and centralized, and does attach a special importance to obedience. This does not mean that it gives obedience a new character, for every religious group can operate only on the same principle. But by way of finding a starting-point, it must be said that a Benedictine vows obedience to the abbot of an autonymous abbey, not to a general or even the Pope, implied as the Papal obedience must be considered. For that matter, every Catholic owes obedience to the Holy Father — under carefully restricted conditions. Thus, he accepts without question the Pope's decisions, when delivered *ex cathedra,* regarding faith and morals, but is completely at liberty when it is a question as to his field of labor. The last is not true in the case of the Jesuit.

We should however observe that the word "obedience" occurs far more often in the Holy Rule of St. Benedict than in the Jesuit Constitutions. Though Ignatius is not quoting directly from any Benedictine source, every particle of the following passage of the Constitutions is assembled from Benedict: "It becomes no less the duty of the subject, when the superior gives, or has given some order, and he thinks there are reasons against it, or difficulties with regard to the thing ordered, to represent to the superior the difficulties or reasons as they appear to him, without inducing him to one course of action more than another, with the intention of following afterward, with a quiet mind, the course that shall be indicated or commanded to him."

That is plain commonsense. While every religious institute prefers unquestioning obedience (such as has to be accorded a military officer), it makes full allowance for the right of "representation." Indeed, though this may be an ideal not always attainable, the Jesuit hope is that the subject will obey as if he, and not the superior, is the one who has given the order.

In addition a great deal of altogether unnecessary horror has been provoked by St. Ignatius' use of such similes as a dead body or a stick in a man's hand. It might help us to get over this if we remembered that St. Francis of Assisi, the very reverse of a martinet, used the same similes, and that they may also be found in St. Basil and still earlier monastic legislators. And if we are thinking of obedience in a military sense, it might be as well, too, to remember Tennyson's famous lines: "Theirs not to reason

why/Theirs but to do and die," and to bear in mind the
fact that if the Light Brigade made its famous charge, this
was due to a couple of wealthy and titled brothers-in-law
in the Crimea being on deplorable relations with one another. Here was a case, if ever there was one, when a
Jesuit's representations would have prevented that appalling blunder.

An even worse misunderstanding regarding Jesuit obedience should be cleared up at the outset. The phrase
obligatio ad peccandum has often been taken by the enemies of the Jesuits as meaning "an obligation to commit
sin," [1] whereas of course it really means that an order may
on rare — very rare — occasions be so decisively framed
as to make the refusal of obedience sinful. (I do not mean,
of course, that the *virtue* of obedience is not subject to
violation.) However, in his Constitutions Ignatius explicitly says, "Obedience is to be rendered when there appears to be no sin." The superior may give an ill-advised
command, and while there may be great merit in carrying
out even such a command, still the right of representation
remains unimpaired, or even becomes a duty. Dr. Harvey,
a recent Protestant biographer of the Saint, makes here
the shrewd comment that prudence is even more desirable in the superior than in the subject.

A final word should be said about obedience in general.
As Archbishop Goodier points out in his little book on the
Society, though the word "obedience" inevitably comes
into the Constitutions, one finds there the word "love"
far more often. St. Francis Xavier used to call the order
"nothing more than a society of Love." This should always be borne in mind as a corrective of popular misconceptions.

[1] Cf. J. H. Pollen, *Saint Ignatius of Loyola,* p. 137.

To any description of the Jesuits as "soldiers," this much must be added: to begin with, Ignatius' background, which may have given rise to the idea, was merely that of other Spaniards of rank; virtually all of them who did not become ecclesiastics adopted the profession of arms. This, however, relates only to a short period of his youth; even then he was never engaged in any long campaign. No doubt he had something of the military mentality, but in this he was not rigidly set.

At the outset there was no idea whatever of founding an order of any kind — for this was something forced by circumstances — but merely an association of friends, inspired, it is true, by Ignatius Loyola, but having no superior. It was nothing like a "muster" that assembled with Ignatius in Italy at the beginning of 1537 merely because it was hoped that they would find a ship in Venice to take them to the Holy Land. All the friends had made a vow to go there, but none had accepted any obligation to perform any agreed-upon task although they had in mind the conversion of the Moslem. Nothing was ever less systematized or organized than this — which of course also means that nothing was less military in its initial stages.

With regard to the vow of obedience to the Pope, though only Jesuits take it explicitly, it had always been implied, at least to the extent that any wish expressed by the Holy Father has great force with Catholics. Thus in the closing years of the sixth century, as St. Gregory the Great was unable, because of having been elected Pope, to go in person as a missionary to England, he induced St. Augustine of Canterbury to take his place. It was so also when thirteen centuries later Leo XIII deflected St. Frances Cabrini from China and sent her instead to the neglected Italian immigrants in the United States. Something of it may even be seen in the case of a girl — she died only recently when she was nearly a centenarian — who knelt at the same Pope's feet urging that help be given to the American Indian and Negro. His answer was, "Why not become a missionary yourself, my child?" That settled the matter for young Katherine Drexel, for she proceeded to throw herself and her immense wealth into this work — a casual suggestion operating as powerfully with her as a positive command.

The vow of obedience taken by the Jesuit is more definite, though papal directives are ordinarily given by immediate superiors rather than by the Holy See itself. Yet as Father James J. Daly, one of the Jesuit friends to whom this little book is inscribed *in memoriam,* has written: "The obedience practiced by a Jesuit is considerably different from that in an army. In the first place, it is more human. It is more human because it is supernatural."

Only so long as one remembers the reservations that have been mentioned — and probably others that have been overlooked — may the Jesuits be rightly said to have a military character. It is true that in some parts of the world they are known as the *Company* and not the *Society* of Jesus, and though the first of these terms does not always and inevitably carry a military significance, such a significance may be given to it under the impression that one is thinking of a military order in the historical sense.

As to other misconceptions. The very word Jesuit acquired in the eighteenth century a sinister tinge, and even now suggests to people who do not have the slightest intention of attacking the order something sly and deceitful — in short, "Jesuitical." More will have to be said about this later. Moreover, even from the days of Ignatius there were pious Catholics who were a bit shocked (or pretended to be) by the presumption, or even the irreverence, of employing the Sacred Name in an official title. The world has long since got over that, though not always in getting over the animosity that the Society was not long in arousing in certain quarters. While this animosity has greatly diminished, it is still something that must be taken into account.

Quite apart from such animosity Ignatius and his friends had in the beginning to meet the objection raised by several influential members of the Roman Curia on the ground that there were already far too many religious orders. Some even went so far as to propose a wholesale suppression of all except the Benedictines, the Franciscans and the Dominicans. Their drastic view did not, as we know, prevail, but had it done so, it would not only have prevented the Jesuits from coming into being but have obliterated the recent clerks regular, together with the Carthusians, the Carmelites, and the Augustinians, not to mention some smaller institutes. Because of the administrative complexities created by having a large number of orders, the argument was made that everything would be more effective if more strictly "streamlined" and simplified. Providentially nothing came of these ideas. Instead, in the wake of the Jesuits, a great many other orders appeared, and in increasing numbers since the seventeenth century.

Broadly it may be said that during the early Middle Ages the terms monk and Benedictine were synonymous. But glorious as had been the Benedictine record, it was already felt during the thirteenth century that a new type of religious was called for — of men who, instead of having the "stability" upon which the Benedictines set

store, should be able to move at their general's direction
from place to place to rescue a world whose ills had
grown too apparent. But whereas in the sixteenth century, St. Francis' friars had fully proved their usefulness,
this could scarcely be said of this little band of Spaniards
(as most of them were) from the University of Paris.
Therefore when Paul III gave them his tentative approbation, he also limited their Company to sixty members, of which small number they were still far short.

Many excellent Catholics of that time considered that
Ignatius was making too radical a departure from all accepted norms. The Company wore no distinguishing religious habit, and they even proposed to abandon the
choral saying of the Divine Office, something that was
considered an essential part of religious life. Besides,
what was the work of this new association? True, they
could preach, but so could any priest who was qualified.
And they could give retreats; but retreats were not exactly new, although usually they were somewhat hap-
hazard until Ignatius appeared upon the scene with a
little book he called the *Spiritual Exercises.*

At the time of such criticisms the nature of the Ignatian
work had hardly manifested itself. For though houses for
the training of other Jesuits were established before long,
schools and colleges for "extern" students did not come
until a little later. The work of those who were to be
master-educationalists was so much in the germ as to be
totally undiscernible; it was not part of the original plan
of Ignatius himself.

Other things that soon developed may be regarded as
only due to a lucky throw but were, of course, a providential seal upon the work of the Company. Among these
must be included the immensely valuable work done by

Laynez and Salmeron at the Council of Trent. Another
of the infant order's achievements was that, even while
the group was so small, it produced in St. Francis Xavier
one of the greatest missionaries the world has ever seen.
In spite of all this there were those who could see no
very evident need for the founding of the Company of
Jesus and reckoned it a most dubious venture.

Later, as was but natural, a good many people, including some of our own time, being aware of how much the
Jesuits had to do with the stemming of the tide of the
Reformation, imagined that it was founded by design for
this very purpose. The matter will be touched upon later,
but at the moment it may be enough to point to the first
great achievements of the Company in countries like
Italy, Spain and Portugal, in which countries the Reformation was not at the time a threat, nor has it ever been.
It is true that elsewhere the order turned out to be perhaps the most formidable weapon in the armory of the
Counter-Reformation, though one must not forget the
contributions made by the Capuchins. But it still is quite
beyond dispute that Ignatius, in launching his enterprise, was not thinking about Luther at all; he had probably never so much as heard the name of that religious
revolutionary until he went to the University of Paris.

What can be said therefore is that Ignatius Loyola appeared at the right or what is called the "psychological"
moment, really by accident, even if the emergence wears
the aspect of design. Though it is true that he established in Rome the German and Roman Colleges which
were to become training grounds for the leaders of the
Counter-Reformation, and sent three of his most valuable men to Germany, Austria, and Bohemia, the major
accomplishments in this respect were the work, not of

Ignatius himself, but of his successors; however one should add that the greatest of the leaders of the Counter-Reformation, St. Peter Canisius, had been trained by Ignatius himself, though not for this specific purpose.

What will have eventually to be gone into more fully is the extraordinary hatred that the Jesuits aroused. I do not for an instant doubt that this hatred redounded to the Jesuits' honor; they were dreaded because of what they achieved. Nevertheless the explanation occasionally offered by Jesuits themselves — or thrown out by some of them as a more or less plausible suggestion — is not very convincing. This is that they were detested by the skeptics of the eighteenth century as much as they were on account of the special vow of obedience they made to the Pope. It seems to me that while the Pope was loathed (when he was not despised) as the embodiment of Catholicism, it was Catholicism — as in the end it was, for many minds, Christianity in any form — which was the target.

In the case of the "philosophers" of the Enlightenment, hatred and contempt came close to fusion. Their keenest mind, Voltaire, was under no illusion when he said of the Jesuits: "Once we get rid of the grenadiers of bigotry, we shall have no trouble with the Infamous Thing." Such people took it for granted that Christianity had almost reached the point of deliquiescence and was being kept alive only as a firmly entrenched and profitable "interest."

In the matter of the hatred mentioned, a few Jesuits admit that what is sometimes described as "Jesuit pride" was the cause of the resentment against them. If so, it may be safely said that this was not, unless in very exceptional instances, pride in the personal sense, but rather pride in the group to which they belonged, something justifiable, though it might have been tactful to conceal it, should it have been felt. Perhaps a better name for the sentiment would be *esprit de corps* and this, good as it usually is, some people thought the Jesuits manifested to an excessive degree. This may be so, but it is hard to see why, if members of a school or club or political party may back one another up, the same privilege should not be extended to Jesuits.

There were, however, reasons why this privilege was sometimes refused. One is that the Jesuits had many rivals among other religious orders, the rivalry being most commonly found (as was only natural) in the case of orders working in a field resembling their own, especially where theological disagreement was found. For instance there was the controversy, which often tended to be acrimonious, between the Jesuits and the Dominicans on the subject of divine grace. This eventually reached such a pass that the Pope was obliged to intervene. Yet instead of delivering a definitive ruling, he issued merely a decision that each order might hold to its own opinion but was not to accuse of heresy those who dissented.

Nor is this all; some jealousy was created by the intensive training of the Jesuits. They have a novitiate of two years instead of one. Then, after the young Jesuit has completed his philosophical studies, he is sent out to teach in a school or college for another two years, and sometimes longer. Finally, after ordination, he undergoes what is called his tertianship, another novitiate during which he has no secular studies but is put through what gives his will a spiritual refurbishing. The result is that it takes several years longer to make a Jesuit than

any other kind of religious. It is possible that this sometimes creates envy among the members of other orders.

There are (or were) other reasons that might explain
the unpopularity from which the Jesuits have suffered,
but these will for the moment suffice. All that remains
to be said in this introduction is, to contradict the idea
that apparently still prevails among some people that
the Jesuits ever upheld the principle that the end justi-
fies the means. A moment's reflection should suffice to
dispose of it. We have here an idea that is not merely at
total variance with Christianity itself (not to mention
the Society of Jesus) but with the common honesty one
expects from all men. At the same time my wish to be
completely honest — even if this involves awkward ad-
missions — leads me to say that not all men *are* honest
and that those in positions of power, whether in the political or ecclesiastical field, have at times succumbed to
a formula which has some immediate advantages, though
it is bound to bring eventual obloquy upon those who
yield to it. Such being the case, it is quite possible that
here and there a Jesuit may (as an individual) have
toyed with this terrible fallacy. If so, I am unable to
think of such a man, whereas at a moment's notice I could
list scores of politicians and lawyers and business men
on the other side. We have here what has been a standing temptation since men appeared upon the earth, and
we may be perfectly sure that this temptation will always remain.

To carry the matter a little further, one may go on to
say that this temptation often operates most powerfully
with men who make lofty professions. For example, we
see it in Cardinal Richelieu and his chief henchman, the
Capuchin Père Joseph, unpopularly known as his Gray

Eminence, when for reasons which they quite sincerely believed to be admirable, they kept Europe plunged in the horrors of the Thirty Years' War even when it might have been terminated. Incidentally, they also preserved the rule of the German Protestant princes, as they believed that Catholicism could be upheld only by France, which meant that the empire of the Catholic Hapsburgs would be weakened. It was all disaster. Yet both Richelieu and Père Joseph have to be considered good men, and the Capuchin somehow managed to combine the practice of mysticism and asceticism with power-politics. Their case seems to me far worse than that of the cynical Thomas Cromwell — Henry VIII himself was characteristically confident that he was irrefragably right in all that he did — and from that point we may come down to the contemplation of the appalling managers of the totalitarian systems of our own time. All that remained was that Hitler should declare that the only measure of right and wrong was the benefit that the state would derive.

To return to Ignatius himself: he began at a time when the need for the reform of the Church was widely recognized, though few knew just where to start upon a task of such complexity. This does not in the least mean that Ignatius was stirred into action to effect the desired reform, for his whole idea at the outset was getting into right relations with God. Following upon this, he conceived the idea of going to the Holy Land to conduct his own kind of crusade. And there he might have remained had not the Franciscan guardians of the Holy Places most plainly told him that the apostolic work he proposed doing among the Moslems would only make the position of all Christians there untenable, as they were allowed to remain only on sufferance. There was nothing but for Ignatius to leave at once.

As soon as he reached Spain again, he was brought to realize that he could accomplish nothing without the education he lacked. Upon this he went back to school, and with small boys or adolescents, until he was sufficiently equipped to attend the universities of Alcalá and Salamanca, from which he passed on to Paris. But already he was armed with the first draft of the *Spiritual Exercises* and these he used in Paris in the formation of his first small band of disciples, inducing all of them to make a vow to go back with him to the Holy Land, apparently hoping that a well-trained group might succeed where a single untrained man had failed. All this shows that he did not have the reform of the Church as his objective, except perhaps in the sense that his followers, who were still without organization of any kind, might accomplish a good deal.

The originality of Ignatius must be found in the *Spiritual Exercises*, in them and in the Jesuit Constitutions, when they were eventually produced. It is clear from both documents, about which more will be said later, that in an age of mysticism — of which the center was Spain — Ignatius, without giving up his first mystical concepts, gave a new application to the formula for joining the contemplative and active modes of life, so succinctly expressed by St. Thomas Aquinas as *Tradere aliis contemplata*. In his plan Martha and Mary were once again to show themselves sisters.

Many Jesuits, including Ignatius himself, have been notable as mystics. But though Ignatius was endowed with mystical gifts he made these serve a practical purpose, as is true in the main of the thousands of men who came to account themselves his sons. In short, the Jesuits laid their immediate stress upon the active life, though this was always to be spiritually nourished, and commonly manifested itself in an asceticism of an interior rather than of an exterior sort.

In this way Ignatius had a great deal to do with that heightening of religious life of which the Church was so sorely in need. But his avowed purpose was the conversion of the individual, by any means that came to hand but basically through the Spiritual Exercises, by which every one of the Jesuits has been moulded. This is something not to be accomplished by getting people to *read* his book, but by making the Exercises under some competent director.

As for Ignatius, once he had been elected, much against his will, as General of the Company of Jesus, he sat for the rest of his life in his little room in Rome, directing the work carried out by his Companions. He preached now and then, and very effectively — in spite of his imperfect command of Italian — and he had a few outside projects, such as the founding of a house of refuge for fallen women. But after he was created General, his chief activity was that of administrator of his spreading Society. Because he kept himself so much out of sight, some surprise was expressed at the movement to canonize him. "Why!" exclaimed one Roman priest, "I always knew that he was a very good man, but I never thought of him as a saint." The opinion would have delighted Ignatius Loyola. He was always one of the most modest of men, and time was needed to reveal the value of what he had begun.

One

The Young Loyola

THOUGH Ignatius Loyola is usually called a Spaniard it should be remembered that, like Francis Xavier, he was really something very different, a Basque. Most of the Basques lived to the south of the Pyrenees, but wherever it was they are not only very unlike the Spaniards in many ways, but unlike all other people. Nobody can speak with any certainty about their origin, as is true also of their language, which has no affinity with any other. Only politically, and at that time relatively recently, had they become part of the Spanish kingdom.

There was, however, this difference between the Loyolas and the Xaviers. Where the Xaviers refused for a number of years to accept the rights claimed by his Majesty of Spain, the Loyola family, because they had kinship with a Spanish duke (as well as for other reasons), put up no resistance to being drawn into the Spanish scheme of things. When war broke out between Spain and France over the ancient kingdom of Navarre, the two families did not take the same side, with the result that the Xaviers, who found themselves among the losers, suffered, though not desperately, on account of their choice, until they came to see that it would be advisable to submit. If the Loyolas and the Xaviers are to be classified as Spaniards, it should be understood in what sense they are to be thought of as such.

16

Ignatius Loyola was born in 1493,[1] the youngest son
of the eight sired by Don Beltram Yánez y Loyola, whose
wife also presented him with five daughters. The family
was neither very rich nor very poor, but its members
were proud of their rank of gentility. Their social standing is indicated by the fact that they were related to the
Duke of Najera. They first appear at the end of the
twelfth century and in 1331 were given a coat-of-arms
by King Alfonso XII of Castile.

The province to which they belonged and where they
had their small castle was Guipúzcoa, a part of the
country where iron ore abounds. It so charges the drink-
ing water that the inhabitants are supposed to have it
in their blood and to derive from it their energy. Be that
as it may, the career of Ignatius Loyola does suggest
that he was largely compact of iron.

At least one of the Loyola brothers became a priest,
and the same might have happened to others had there
been a sufficiency of well-endowed benefices obtainable. As Ignatius was not at all pious, or at any rate not
pious enough to think of the cloister, he became a soldier
—arms being one of the very few professions fitting to
a gentleman—and attached himself to the entourage of
his kinsman the duke. However, as this was not a time
when great wars had to be fought, the Moors at Granada
having been defeated and expelled about the time of
Ignatius' birth, his duties were largely nominal, or rather
decorative, so that he had a good deal of time on his
hands.

He spent it as might be imagined, in looking as grand

[1] Père Dudon, the best of his biographers, says, however, that this
date seems to be indicated by inference; there are no definite records.
In their absence 1491 is more often named as the year of his birth and
is the date preferred by the Jesuit editors of the *Monumenta Historica*.

as his rather diminutive height would permit, in gambling, fighting duels and in casual love affairs. We also hear of his trying his hand at poetry, but none of his compositions have survived, and it may be safely surmised that this was not much to the world's loss. Certainly the hymn he wrote out in the *Spiritual Exercises* — one still often sung in Catholic churches — was not by him, though it was long thought to be that. The poems actually produced by him were probably addressed to this or that of his light loves, or may even have been made use of for several ladies in turn. That he did have something to repent in his conduct we know from the confidences he gave in later life to his secretary Polanco. Still without questioning the truth of these, it is unlikely that he was much of a libertine; certainly no mark of what happened at this time was left upon him. In all probability Ignatius Loyola was better rather than worse than other idle young soldiers.

This need not be taken as a mere guess, for it emerges that, whatever earthy love affairs there were, Ignatius Loyola was also a good deal of a romantic. His great love, so he himself says, was a lady so exalted as to be quite unattainable, and to whom in all likelihood he did not venture so much as to speak of what was in his heart. Just who this lady was has been a matter of speculation. All kinds of candidates have been put forward, including the beautiful Germaine de Foix, the second wife of King Ferdinand, the Princess Joan who married the King of Naples or — which sounds rather improbable — her daughter Joan. Perhaps it is not without significance that Catalina, the wife of King John III of Portugal, later took a keen interest in the Jesuits, as comes out from the fact that King John insisted in having some Jesuits sent as missionaries to Goa in India.[1] There is really nobody else that one can think of, unless Ignatius was exaggerating, which was not his way. Who the lady was does not matter very much; what does matter is that a romantic, versifying young officer whose heart was set upon a personage of this sort is not one who would have been a profligate, even though he may not have refused to make an easy conquest that came his way.

Ignatius had some reputation as a duelist, for his courage was remarked as also his swordsmanship. One hears of the fiery fellow once getting angry with a whole band of soldiers and of his chasing them, blade in hand, down a hill. But they came against him again, and Ignatius afterward thought he would certainly have been killed, had not another young officer—a gay spark like himself, though destined to become a bishop—put both arms around him and held him until the soldiers were safely out of the way. One suspects that they took the affray not very seriously but rather as a joke, for obviously, despite the presence of the future bishop, they could have surrounded Ignatius and run him through. But the incident reveals what was not unlike the foolhardy courage he was to show at Pamplona. It also reveals that the prudence which was one of his most notable characteristics in later life was masked by a courage kept under rigid control.

One glimpse we get of Ignatius as a soldier is very revealing. It was that once, when the soldiers of his command proposed pillaging a town, Ignatius told them sternly that this would not be "the act of either a Chris-

[1] Father Leturia, who wrote in 1936, supports this view, which I also suggested in the life of Francis Xavier I published the same year. Fulöp-Miller, however, holds that the lady must have been Germaine de Foix, which Leturia considers quite impossible.

tian or a gentleman." Warfare was coming to be conducted with courtesy, though it suffered a throwback in
the seventeenth century; pillaging was far from the
Ignatian concept of how enemies ought to comport
themselves. Even during the Thirty Years' War, as one
may gather from the celebrated painting by Velasquez,
"The Surrender of Breda," the ideal of courtly military
grace was still kept, slight as may have been the usual
practice.

The only other glimpse that need be given here of
Ignatius as a soldier is his last appearance in this capacity. It was when, as one of the defenders of Pamplona
against the French, he refused to surrender, though all
the other officers were in favor of this. His stubborn
valor was the occasion of his subsequent conversion, for
as he stood upon the ramparts a cannon ball hit his right
leg, shattering the bone completely, while the other leg
was wounded by flying masonry. It so happened that
among the besiegers were two of the elder brothers of
Francis Xavier — Francis himself at this date being a little
too young to bear arms — and while it is not very likely
that, as officers, either would have discharged the cannon,
they might well have given the order to fire. However, it is
not necessary to speculate on this point. When Ignatius
Loyola was brought down all resistance was broken. The
French and their Navarrese allies streamed in and all
was over.

Put in another way, it might be said that after Ignatius had recovered from his wounds, he could have continued as a soldier, as it would not much matter to an
officer that he was left with a limp. In that event the
world would never have heard of him. Actually the fall
of Pamplona closed a chapter in his life. His broken leg

was what eventually led to his conversion and to the founding of the Company of Jesus.

It has been said that Ignatius Loyola was not a great reader of books. But perhaps this should be qualified; during his more idle moments up to this time he was given, every now and then, to the reading of the kind of fantastic romances that addled what poor Don Quixote had of brains. In later years, though Ignatius gave evidence of reading more solid works, he never came to be what is called a bookish man. Nor is this the least surprising: reading is a taste that one has to acquire in youth, if at all.

But on his sickbed in Loyola Castle Ignatius soon became desperately bored. The French who had taken Pamplona showed all due military courtesy to their valiant enemy by sending him in a litter, borne by their own men, to his ancestral home, and there it did not take Ignatius long — if he had ever been in doubt about it — to be sure that he had many dreary weeks to lie in bed before his fractured bone mended. Presumably now and then relatives or friends dropped in, and his sisters brought him his meals, but except for an hour or two every day he was left completely alone, something very hard for anybody without inner resources to endure.

At Loyola Castle there were not many books, for these were rare in those days, and none of the members of his family was much addicted to reading. However, at his request a search was made, with perhaps inquiries among the neighboring gentry, who were no more bookish than themselves. As a result two books were eventually produced. These were a life of Christ by Ludolph of Saxony and an adaptation or condensation of the two big volumes written by the Dominican Jacobus de Voragine in the thirteen century and known as *The Golden Legend*.[1] The work had been widely circulated, but as it had to be copied by hand, the labor of producing it had been lightened by cutting down the contents and reissuing it as the *Flos Sanctorum*. Upon the whole it was the best collection of the Lives of the Saints available, and it was certainly the best collection to place in the hands of Ignatius. Even the fact that it was occasionally rather mythical helped, for that made it not too unlike the romances that hitherto had been Loyola's favorite reading. At all events it had a tremendous effect upon him. If the worthy Dominican had written it for no other reader than the future founder of the Society of Jesus, his labors would have been well repaid.

Ignatius had hitherto taken up books of this sort with languid interest, if at all. But he was in the mood when a man will read anything to give his mind some occupation, and though he must have been fairly well acquainted with the Gospel story — at least in its main lines — he was now able to meditate upon the significance of much that a young man, a bit lax in conduct though firm in his faith, had never before considered in this close way. Yet it would seem that, at this stage, of the two books it was the *Flos Sanctorum* that impressed him most deeply.

Its initial impact upon him was not of the loftiest sort. It aroused in him feelings of emulation — good enough of course but only a preliminary to something better. In

---

[1] The English translation by Granger Ryan and Helmut Ripperger published in 1941 I have before me; there is another in several volumes in the Temple Classics. The work, which was one of the "best sellers" of the Middle Ages has a good deal of charm, but it need hardly be said it does not begin to meet the standards of scientific biography.

particular Ignatius was stirred by the lives of St. Francis
and St. Dominic, many friars of whose orders he must
have often encountered. In those days he would have
thought that their ideals did not have much to do with
a young officer in the army, given to whiling away his
free hours with dice and now and then a little wench-
ing.

Loyola's reading of the lives of these saints made him
say to himself: "If they could do this, I could do the
same and more." He eventually proved that in truth he
could equal their deeds, but it was an emulous spirit
which at that time made him harbor such thoughts.
The first and absolutely indispensable thing was that he
become a vastly better Christian, and this as yet had
not occurred to him as a goal.

Meanwhile he exhibited qualities which one has to
place in the natural order but which showed an astonishing fortitude. When the surgeons set his broken leg
the operation was very painful, but he endured it without allowing a groan to escape or a quiver to appear on
his face. That of course was something that many a
wounded soldier in those days before the use of anes-
thetics had to undergo, though few of them displayed the
Ignatian impassivity. Even so, this was not enough. The
surgeons of those days, or those who could be summoned
to Loyola Castle, were not very skilled as compared with
the bone specialists of our own time. Therefore when the
leg was set it was discovered that a bit of bone ob-
truded; not much, but enough to prevent Ignatius from
wearing again the high, tight-fitting boots that smartly
accoutered officers then affected. No doubt he could
have gone before his company in footgear of a less
fashionable sort, but this he did not want to do, as it

would necessitate his explaining his predicament. So though the doctors warned him that to saw away that scrap of bone would be more painful than all that had gone before, Ignatius insisted that it be removed, and stoically endured his agony. We cannot but call his fortitude admirable, yet its object was only to obtain a more fashionable appearance — perhaps to make him out a better figure in the eyes of foolish women. In later life he must have reckoned himself more foolish than the silliest girl among them. In the event his anguish was to no purpose; never again did he wear the smart military boots, and after undergoing all this he still limped a little.

Nobody would have thought of Ignatius Loyola at this time as a great religious leader. And while his reading of the books he had borrowed no doubt did him much good at the time, the greater part of the good came from subsequent memory. We might say that he had already become a better Christian; we cannot say that he was now a saint or even had any ambition to become one.

Then suddenly the unexpected and decisive thing happened. He had been wounded at Pamplona at the end of May 1521, and he was carried to Loyola Castle a few days later. There he lay on his sickbed until August 15th, the feast of the Assumption, though he seems to have been able to get up after a couple of months and hobble to Mass at the chapel of the little castle. Yet at Mass he did not exhibit such an access of piety that it was marked. But on Our Lady's feast day she appeared to him as he lay awake at night, and in her arms was the Infant Jesus. From the very explicit account he gave of the matter in 1555 to Father Gonzales de Camara, one gathers that no word was spoken, but

Ignatius saw the vision with crystal clarity.[1] He positively testified that from that moment he never again gave the slightest consent to any impure thought. He added to Camara with true Ignatian caution: "From this effect, the incident may be judged to have been of God," but he did not venture to be positive about this. The conversion of Ignatius Loyola, except in so far as it was a process that called for further development, may be dated from that August night in 1521.

As it is my intention to be as brief as possible in the opening biographical chapter of this book, perhaps only one other thing needs to be said here. Though Ignatius Loyola had not so much as heard of Martin Luther, and definitely did not found the Company of Jesus to stem the tide of Protestantism, it was during the selfsame months when the young soldier was convalescing at home that Luther was in hiding at Wartburg Castle. He had been taken there by an "arranged" abduction, and in this sacred spot where St. Elizabeth of Hungary had lived with her youthful husband, the Landgrave of Thuringia, Luther translated part of the Bible — after all, a notable achievement — and had thrown his inkwell at the Devil, which confirms what is believed of his neurotic temperament. In this coincidence of dates, which is exact almost to the day, we may be permitted to see that in Ignatius Loyola there was being providentially prepared the instrument that the age needed. Of this Ignatius was of course quite unconscious, however conscious he was that all happenings come into being because of God's design.

[1] Though Ignatius may perhaps not be among the greatest visionaries, he did have visions from time to time all through his life.

Two

Manresa

Since the strange coincidence of dates regarding Luther at the Wartburg and Loyola at the family castle has been mentioned, perhaps the matter should be continued just a moment longer. We know that it was on March 1, 1522, that Luther left his hiding-place for Wittenburg. Though we do not know the precise day when Ignatius left Loyola, with his home retreat at an end, it must have been somewhere very near the same time. Without attaching any special significance to these dates — for if there was any it was known only to God — we may at least be permitted to think the coincidence very striking.

The very first thing that Ignatius did, by way of starting his new life, was to make a pilgrimage. One might have expected him, especially as he had been until recently a soldier, to make his way to Compostella, the most famous and, indeed, the national shrine of Spain, for it was at Compostella that St. James, Spain's patron saint, had his tomb. But the thought of doing this never seems to have entered Loyola's head. From this one may infer several things, one being that Ignatius was not thinking in merely Spanish terms, another that Compostella was near the Atlantic, whereas Ignatius wished to go in the direction of the Mediterranean for we know that he was

already thinking of a pilgrimage to Jerusalem. But perhaps the more immediate and decisive reason was that
he knew he would find at Compostella a mob of pilgrims
milling around, and that his first objective was to find a
place of quiet retirement. He wished to rival the saints
in austerity and penance and to carry farther the train
of thought already begun at Loyola Castle.

It may well be that he had already had a glimpse of
Montserrat, or knew of its sanctuary to Our Lady; at
any rate, it was there that he made his way. On arriving
his first care was to make a general confession of his
sins; for this he prepared by three days of self-examina-
tion. Then, giving his handsome clothing to the poor, he
put on a garment of sackcloth reaching to his feet, and
after a night spent in watching at the altar and in the
morning receiving Communion he left for Barcelona, taking — in order to avoid recognition — a roundabout way
through "a town called Manresa."

To make the pilgrimage to Jerusalem he had sought the
needed permission of Rome, but this was delayed and, in
addition, a plague descended upon Barcelona. So the few
days Ignatius had planned spending in Manresa grew in
the end to ten months. During this time he, the *hidalgo*,
lived by begging his bread and practicing the greatest
penances and austerities. He was sheltered by turns in a
hospice for the poor and in a cell put at his disposal by
the Dominican friars within whose church he was daily
present at high Mass as well as vespers and compline. But
the mountains thereabout had also a number of caves in
the craggy cliffs where he could meditate undisturbed.
Possibly the germ of his famous Spiritual Exercises was
already at work, but if so, it could only have been in a
vague and rudimentary form. More probably he sought

the cave near the little town of Manresa to pray there in
solitude; it is unlikely that he went there to write a book,
but we do know that a book was one of the results.

Certainly the form and composition of the Exercises
reflect his own spiritual experiences at Manresa, for there
before obtaining the peace he sought by prayer, austerities and contemplation, he was consumed by the most
troublesome scruples, and indeed, we are told, thought
even of suicide. It was when this ordeal was finally
passed that his book began to take shape, at least in his
own mind.

How far the *Spiritual Exercises* could have begun to
take written form we do not know. What we do know is
that even after this period of retirement — brief though
the book is in its final form — the *Spiritual Exercises* was
constantly retouched and recast for another twenty years
before Ignatius was satisfied.

About the *Exercises* it is sometimes imagined that they
were written in the cave to which Ignatius retired. It is
quite true that Manresa was a spot where he could pray
and meditate without fear of interruption, but it seems
unlikely that Ignatius did any writing there, unless he
had been supplied with a table and a chair. While it is
not impossible that this happened, I suggest that at most
Ignatius made a few notes, scrawled rather illegibly on
his knee or on a bit of paper spread on a handy boulder,
and that he copied these out when he got to his cell at
the Dominican friary where he was staying. If so, all
that could have eventuated was a very rough first draft.

This need not be considered a guess, when we remember how painfully Ignatius composed,[1] even after he had

---

[1] This remained true to the end, and despite the thousands of letters
which he wrote from Rome to the members of his order. His beautiful
script was admired later, but it never made him a fluent writer.

attended three universities and had, in Rome, all the conveniences for writing at his disposal. Moreover, Ignatius was as yet only at the beginning of his new life, and was a man without what is ordinarily understood as education, as well as without the spiritual training of which he was later to give so full a proof.

Nevertheless the importance of Loyola's stay at Manresa must not be reckoned at less than enormous. It was at Manresa that he thought out the *Spiritual Exercises*. not as a book but as a means he first used upon himself by way of setting his own spiritual life in order. Only later, and after he had more fully developed his method, did it become a means of his doing something for the spiritual life of other people. The *Exercises* did not appear in their final form until around 1540, during which time they were revised and added to as Ignatius progressed in the knowledge of God and of human nature.

In a later chapter it will be discussed what, if any, contributions were made to the work by the various religious orders with which Ignatius came into contact at Montserrat. There are some Jesuits who take the ground that he drew so very slightly from other sources that these sources may be treated as virtually negligible. But there are critics — the majority of whom are, naturally enough, of other religious institutes — who do their best to represent the *Exercises* as being little more than a compilation, one might almost say an anthology. They start with what seems to be a very strong point: Ignatius does not strike one as having a very original mind. Against this, we must remember that the later Jesuit Constitutions constitute so radical a departure from what had come to be accepted as the norms of religious life as to be startling, to some even a bit shocking. One can only say that, slowly and cautiously as the mind of Ignatius may have moved, it did, after all, conceive an idea more original than any introduced by St. Francis or St. Dominic, superior though their minds may have been in some respects to his own. If that is true of the Constitutions, there is no reason why originality should be denied to the *Exercises.*

Yet Loyola's originality must have been of a very peculiar sort, if it was at once able to bring forward things so novel but in such a way as to seem to everybody unobtrusive and to all but a relative few nonexistent. One thinks of the general consideration, which has undeniable force, that absolute originality is wellnigh inconceivable. Doubtless all "new" ideas are not, strictly speaking, new at all, but only appear to be so because they are presented in a novel arrangement. Any one mind, however lofty or subtle, is nearly always — perhaps one might say *always* without qualification — kindled by another, or has borrowed something from another, even in its most "original" moments. This is a question that will have to be gone into later, but the mind of Ignatius was of the kind to be affected by the books he had read.

In spite of this, it is amply evident that Ignatius wrote nothing at Manresa or anywhere else that he did not make his own by brooding over it with the most concentrated attention. But finally there is the pragmatic test: there is nothing like the *Exercises,* either as they stand or in the unparalleled effect they have had. One can imagine somebody writing another *Imitation* (though this may need the straining of the imagination); one simply cannot picture another man producing anything comparable to the *Spiritual Exercises.* Therefore it might be as well to drop at once all preconceived notions regarding this book.

While at Manresa Ignatius thought for a while of joining the Carthusians, a clear indication that he felt a strong attraction to the contemplative life. It is providential that further thought and prayer led him to abandon this idea. In a Carthusian cell (which is close to being a hermitage) he could of course have become a saint — though the Carthusians carefully avoid seeking the canonization of any of their members; but while he might have prayed for the conversion of mankind, he would have been debarred from working for it in any active way. Though there is not the slightest reason to suppose that Ignatius, at this stage, dreamed that the Exercises would be useful for anybody besides himself, he did before long come to perceive the serviceability of the instrument he had forged, which was why he spent so many years in sharpening it until it had the keenest possible edge. Whatever the reasons that operated — they were probably many more than have been indicated — Ignatius decided not to join the Carthusians, or any order at all. This must not be taken to mean that he envisaged, even in the dimmest outline, what eventually came into being as the Company of Jesus — for such an idea did not occur to him until many years later — but merely that he felt that it was God's will for him that he should hold himself completely unattached until he received definite directions from on high.

I shall say no more about Manresa, reserving the rest of my remarks for a later chapter. Only this much needs to be added here: Ignatius kept very much to himself, and in fact spent much of the time in his cave. But we know that, in addition to the religious communities there, he became acquainted with a number of pious women, who sought him out, pressing upon him small gifts of which they saw he stood in need but would never ask for. Just what went on in his mind we must gather chiefly from the *Spiritual Exercises,* though what he at last allowed to appear must have been in many respects different from the rough first draft that came out of his visit to Montserrat.

It may be safe to say this much: the conversion that had occurred on August 15th of the previous year was being rounded out. Ignatius bent all his energies to examining every nook and cranny of his soul, extirpating every frailty he could find. Above all—and this must never be forgotten, as it became a cardinal principle with him—he sought to learn God's will as to what he should do with his life. He had begun to hold himself unattached, convinced that it did not matter in the least what work he did so long as it was the work to which he was called.

Three
Pilgrimage

THERE NOW COMES an episode in the life of Ignatius Loyola which for most people of our time will be all but inexplicable. In February of 1523 he set out for the Holy Land. Though this chapter is titled "pilgrimage" more than pilgrimage was really involved. About that sort of thing, which had been going on all through the Middle Ages, we have been left a few accounts by the pilgrims themselves, the most recent of which is Miss Prescott's amusing and vivid *Friar Felix at Large*. After Christendom had suffered its ignominious repulse in the Crusades, an arrangement was reached with the Moslem victors (for presumably they must be called that) under which Christians would be permitted to visit their Holy Places — some of which were holy to Islam, too — but under restrictions that were rigorously enforced. The Saracens were well aware that the idea of the crusade had not been abandoned; nor was it indeed really abandoned until in the seventeenth century it became evident to everybody that Christianity was permanently divided.

Yet Ignatius Loyola set forth not so much as a pilgrim as a crusader, one attempting what was virtually a one-man crusade. He wished of course to see with his own eyes, and for his personal spiritual benefit, the places where his Saviour had lived, and though he rarely, if ever, attempts to describe any of them in his Exercises, he very frequently asks his retreatants to attempt what he called "the composition of place," which was the putting of these places before them in imagination. But Ignatius was not doing the ordinary pious act, a mere pilgrimage; he wished also to convert the Moslems. This apostolic task was perhaps the most difficult that he could have chosen, but it is very revealing that he began his career in this way. Nor was the idea so absurd as it might seem at first sight, for Ignatius was counting upon God, to whom all things are possible. And the instrument he meant to employ was the Spiritual Exercises, something that might profitably be made by people of almost any religion. Ignatius, having come from Spain, must often have encountered Moors and have been made aware that there are wide tracts of belief that they held in common with Christians.

However, there was the language difficulty, though this might have been partially overcome through the use of an interpreter until Ignatius had himself learned the speech of the Moslems. But as things, not very surprisingly, turned out, Ignatius was imperfectly understood and succeeded only in giving offense. At any rate the Franciscan Fathers, who were the guardians of the Holy Places, took alarm and advised Ignatius to leave, which was equivalent to an order. They knew these people much better than the pilgrim could and were aware how very touchy they were. After all, Christian visitors were admitted only on sufferance, and the Franciscans may well have feared that they themselves would be ejected on account of Loyola's apostolic zeal.

By February, 1524, therefore, we find Ignatius back in Barcelona, after having been away for about a year.

Though to all seemingly he had accomplished nothing
except the good he had derived for himself, he had by
no means given up the hope of evangelizing the Holy
Land. A little over ten years later, when Ignatius and
his first permanent group of disciples at the University
of Paris took their vows at Montmartre, though they
were not at that time a religious order or had any intention of constituting themselves one, the only vow they
took, except for the ordinary vows of chastity and poverty (but not of obedience, since they had as yet no
superior) was that of going to the Holy Land. By then,
however, they may have been thinking merely of a pilgrimage, as Ignatius had already learned that missionary
work among the Moslems would not be tolerated.

Ignatius arrived back in Spain quite penniless, but
instead of going to Loyola Castle, where his family,
though not at all wealthy, would have done something
for him, he remained at the port at which he landed,
Barcelona. Or rather, he settled there, after making a
brief visit to Montserrat.

All this is not so unaccountable as at first glance it might
seem. By now Ignatius had been brought to recognize
that if he was to do any solid spiritual work, he must
first get an education. This was something much more
easily obtainable in a large city than in a little castle in
a country district. At Loyola, Ignatius might, it is true,
have obtained the rudiments, but he was thinking of a
good deal more than that.

Yet Ignatius was not, even in 1524, what can be called
illiterate, for we hear of his early versifying and we know
that he read books now and then; and to have written
the Exercises, even in the roughest sort of rough drafts,
must have called for an education at least as good as the

ordinary *hidalgo* of those days would have possessed. But to go on to studies of a higher sort meant, as he knew, that he would have to begin at the bottom again. Even an elementary education involved learning some Latin, and though Ignatius must have once studied its elements, by now, as he was over thirty, most of what he had once known had faded from his mind.

At Barcelona the town council appears to have been more progressive than in most places, for it had gone to the trouble of establishing free public schools, or at least *a* school, open to anybody, and of engaging competent teachers. Ignatius was grateful to the teacher he had, and there must have been good reason, for he never forgot him. This man's name was Jerome Ardeval, and in his classes Ignatius Loyola, once a captain in the army and of excellent family, used also to associating — at least to some extent and one would even gather rather intimately — with members of the court, sat with young boys to learn his lessons.

His attendance was to the edification of Ardeval, who was naturally interested in such a student, so eager to learn but who found it hard at his age to get into his head the instruction that presented no difficulty to younger and nimbler minds. Moreover, though Ignatius was, in his way, a genius, he had probably never been very clever in the more conventional fashion. Ardeval perceived what was the handicap and hit upon the right expedient of giving the mature man private lessons. Ignatius thankfully promised that he would never fail to give full attention to his teacher, so long as he could find means of supporting life at Barcelona.

What he needed by way of shelter was provided by a woman named Iñes Pascual, whose husband kept a small

shop in the center of the city, she and her husband living
in an apartment on the second floor. Above this was a
loft, fifteen feet long and thirteen wide but only five
feet high. This had served as the bedroom of the Pas-
cuals' young son. But though Ignatius was invited to
take his meals at the family table, he preferred to beg
for them, subsisting mainly on bread and water, so that
every day with him was a fast day.

Not content with this, Ignatius went in for the kind of
physical penances which he largely discarded in later life,
thinking them to be upon the whole a mistake. He also
discouraged their practice among his followers, without, however, actually forbidding them. But he was at
the beginning of his spiritual life, and such things seemed
appropriate, especially to one nurtured in the Spanish
tradition. The meager fare must have been detrimental
to study, but though asceticism of this variety was drawing to an end, it was not until St. Francis de Sales wrote
nearly a couple of generations later that those who
aspired to sanctity began to be disabused of notions that
had long held the field. Ignatius, though he worked
within a narrower circle in his time and had for a long
while a much smaller audience than did the writer of
The Introduction to the Devout Life, has a right to be
credited with having anticipated much that the famous
Bishop of Geneva was going to say. The conclusions to
which he eventually came were the result of his own
experiences in the matter.

For the concepts he entertained during this earlier
period of his life Ignatius should in no way be blamed.
He had read something about them in the *Flos Sanctorum,* so, as he had no guide at hand, it is not to be
wondered at that there may have been some errors in

his first mode of life. But it is possible that by them he undermined his constitution and they may, in part, account for his dying in 1556, still a relatively young man. Not only was his fare of the most meager sort, but he declined using the bed provided for him unless he had removed its mattress, or else slept on the floor.[1] As if this was not enough, Ignatius made holes in the soles of his shabby shoes — which he may have thought of as a penance for being formerly so proud of his military boots — and kept constantly enlarging those holes, till by the time that winter arrived hardly anything was left except the uppers. On top of everything else, he used to discipline himself with a chain.

It would be inaccurate to say too emphatically that Ignatius came to the point of fixed opposition to physical asceticism of every kind, but his later views come out in a letter written more than twenty years later to the now canonized Duke of Gandia, when that great personage[2] had joined the newly founded Jesuits. This contains the words: "We ought to love and cherish the body in so far as it is obedient and helpful to the soul, for with such obedience and assistance the soul can the better dispose itself to serve and praise our Creator and Lord." He there says plainly: "I would be for avoiding altogether any form of it [penance] that could cause a single drop of blood to appear." Instead he advocates the seek-

[1] One must not make too much of this, however; my charming, learned, eccentric and holy friend, the English Dominican, Father Vincent McNabb, also slept on the floor, and yet worked vigorously to the end of his eighty-odd years. In spite of this it is surely not unreasonable to maintain that one should give due care to one's body, if one is to give one's best to God's service.

[2] A great-grandson of Pope Alexander VI and also of King Ferdinand. This gave him a kinship with Henry VIII, through that King's marriage to Katherine of Aragon.

ing of spiritual gifts. It was not of course that Ignatius ever came to consider physical mortifications wrong, but he more highly valued those that were interior. He had learned by personal experience that if a man was to do his work well, he should do his utmost to preserve his health; and what were Jesuits called to if not to work for the greater glory of God?

At the same time one must not forget what appears in the *Exercises* in the form in which nearly twenty years later they left his hands. There he advocates "chastising the flesh, by causing it sensible pain" and approves the wearing of a hair shirt, cords, or chains around the body. He makes the proviso, however, that the penance "should be sensible to the flesh, and not penetrate the bone, so that pain and not sickness, be the result. For which purpose it seems to be more convenient to discipline oneself with small cords, which cause pain exteriorly, than to do so in any other way, from which may result any notable injury to the health." The statement was very moderate, especially for those pre-Salesian days, for it is clear that while not condemning more drastic physical mortifications, Ignatius considers that usually the employment of a scourge should suffice.

It is worth remarking that Ignatius during these early years was befriended by women. Possibly this was partly due to his being still young and having a dapper, or maybe even an aristocratic way with him despite his shabbiness. Women, being usually more observant than men, knew by simply glancing at him that he was a remarkable person. Mingled with this was the fact that kind feminine hearts went out in pity to one obviously in need, especially when they caught glimpses of his holiness. Though we do not hear that Loyola at this time accepted any money from Iñes Pascual, not long afterward, when he went on to the university and was obliged to have funds, penurious as was his mode of life, he did accept small sums from patrons, and the majority of these were women.

Nevertheless, Ignatius never had a close woman friend, as was the case of St. Francis of Assisi and St. Clare, or St. Francis de Sales and St. Jane Frances de Chantal, or St. Vincent de Paul whose right hand was St. Louise de Marillac (along with half the other noble ladies of Paris). Ignatius, on the contrary, while he was of course always very polite and charming with women, was a bit "distant" with them. This may be due to some extent to his memory of his unregenerate youth, but he was always careful not to get into anything even remotely resembling intimate terms. Moreover he later discovered that a woman who had done him a signal service might expect the kind of recognition he was not prepared to give. In plainer and blunter terms, women were capable of making themselves something of a nuisance. He therefore would never so much as listen to any suggestion that the Jesuits have a female branch, and ordinarily did not like the idea that any of his sons should be so much as a confessor to a convent of nuns.

In this no doubt there was commonsense, as his commonsense also saw that members of the Society might be obliged to avail themselves of the good offices of powerful people (women as well as men) for permissions that were indispensable if they were to perform their work. It was only that Ignatius feared those who were officious and demanding, yet who did not contribute much to what the Society had to do. I do not imagine that all his regulations on this point are now very rigidly enforced, or are often called for, but his rules were necessary while the new Society was still in a more or less experimental stage.

The stay of Ignatius at Barcelona lasted just over two years. The period can hardly be regarded as very exciting, important though it was, as during that time he was largely occupied in brushing up a Latin that had grown somewhat rusty since he was a boy, and of course in acquiring a good deal more than he had ever known. All this he rightly regarded as indispensable, if he was to be able to do the work to which he felt called. We must therefore applaud the dogged way in which he beat his declensions and conjugations into his head, along with some general reading of the simpler classical authors.

What must never be forgotten is how Ignatius forged slowly on, painful inch by inch, always with his goal in sight, a goal which steadily grew clearer, even if he still did not fully realize to what all this would lead. Never once did he deviate in the slightest. We may suppose that under a private tutor—who seems himself to have been a rather remarkable man—Ignatius made more progress than would have been attainable in four years in a classroom. Yet we will get the whole picture wrong if we think of Ignatius as being brilliant, for that he never was. Without question he was a genius, but the terms are by no means interchangeable. Ignatius Loyola does not need me to describe him as one of the world's formative intellects. His power resided in the firmness with which he grasped a few ideas of the utmost importance, in that and in a will of iron.

Four

Preparation

LORD MACAULAY, in a famous essay in which, somewhat bewilderedly, he tried to account for the survival of the Catholic Church, and indeed some advantages he had to admit that it has over the Protestant system, had to fall back, among other ideas, to that of the Catholic Church's ability to make use even of its untrained enthusiasts. Without pausing to examine this interesting suggestion, it must be said that Ignatius was not what one ordinarily understands to be the enthusiastic type; at any rate he had gradually acquired the self-training that brought enthusiasm under the control of a strict judgment. Moreover, though Ignatius was a more or less untrained person at the time of his conversion, he soon recognized that fact and spent a number of weary years in remedying it. He even came to see that for his distinctive work — which we would not too inaccurately describe as the giving of the Spiritual Exercises to those who desired perfection — it was absolutely necessary to have a high pitch of intellectual as well as spiritual training. It was therefore an essential part of his plan that he prepare himself by means of attending a university.

He knew moreover that the first drafts of the Exercises he had made in 1522 were not quite satisfactory, and he spent twenty years in revising them over and over again.

Yet he never regarded the Exercises as something to be concocted out of other books, and in fact never became what is called a "bookish" person. The Exercises remained basically the fruit of his personal experience, and anything he read was relatively useless to him until he had so thoroughly absorbed it as to make it his own. This is why his critics often go grievously astray in their search for derivations and sources. These no doubt are there, but they are hard to discover, because before they were usable at all, they had to become part of Loyola's own originality. Education was, however, essential to him because he saw that his mind had to be trained. A reason almost as important as this was that he perceived the Exercises could be administered with much benefit only by other trained minds.

This was not so much because he addressed himself primarily to men who had gone through a university, for while it is true that he found his first permanent disciples among men of this type, he was not looking for what the world commonly regards as superior people, and least of all for dessicated pedants. Again he was taught by experience, for when he went to Alcalá in the summer of 1526 the three men who came from Barcelona to aid him in his labors to help souls were even less learned than himself and most of those who gathered around him to be taught how to examine their conscience and to make a meditation were women, many of whom were of a somewhat hysterical disposition. Perhaps the teaching he administered did them some good, and this teaching must have been based upon the Exercises; but it was not long before he came to perceive that these women, however well-intentioned, were not quite the material he was seeking.

If he commenced his own higher studies at Alcalá, this may have been because its university, which had been founded in 1510 by the great Cardinal Jiminez de Cisneros, enjoyed a reputation second only to that of the older Salamanca. It was there, by the way, that the famous Complutensian Polyglot Bible was being prepared. While we might well be very wrong in imagining that this particular project had anything to do with the decision taken by Ignatius, it is noteworthy that Erasmus, because of various delays that attended the publication of the Cardinal's version, succeeded in getting to the wire with his notes on the New Testament only a few months before Cisneros. What Erasmus gave to the world created so immense a sensation that it almost came to be taken as the seed-plot of the Reformation, much to the disgust of its author. For while, being a man of considerable vanity, he delighted in his celebrity, nothing annoyed him more than to be described as the egg from which Luther was hatched. Yet there was more than a little truth in this, good as his intentions were, and we know that later on Ignatius conceived a deep dislike and distrust of him on account of such works as the *Militis Christiani* (1504) and the *Moriae Encomium* (1512), though the second of these was tossed out as a *jeu d'esprit* in the house of his bosom friend St. Thomas More.

It must be remembered that Ignatius was a reformer of a very different stripe from Erasmus (or even the gay-hearted More). It takes all kinds of men to make a world, and the intensity of Ignatius, though it did not make him solemn, made him unable to see how wit— especially of the Erasmian variety—might do any service to religion. The Jesuit attitude was subsequently expressed by St. Peter Canisius, *Utinam Erasmus in gram-*

matica semper; numquam in theologia. There are many instances when one is obliged to admire a writer for his style or his learning, and still be obliged to reprehend much that he says.

Yet Ignatius was not lacking in sardonic humor. There was an example of this when the ecclesiastical authorities at Alcalá grew alarmed at some of his activities and ordered him under a mild form of imprisonment for six weeks while they examined his teaching. They did in the end command him and the friends who followed him not to dress alike, as this might make people think them members of a religious order, but Juan Rodríguez de Figueroa, vicar-general to the Archbishop of Toledo, told him, after examination, that no error had been discovered in his teaching, and added, "If they had found heresy, they would have burned you." To this Ignatius answered with demure aplomb, "As they would have burned you, had they found you a heretic." What reply could be made to such a rejoinder?

The studies Ignatius made at Alcalá were not very satisfactory, the reason being that he was in such a hurry to master all available branches of knowledge — to make up for his having begun much later than most students — that he mastered relatively little. He still had to acquire a method, and after his brush with the suspicious local ecclesiastics, he felt that he would do better by moving elsewhere. He had catechized children; he had talked to little groups of pious but, one fears, not always very well balanced women; but he had accomplished not much more in the field of his apostolate. One could hardly expect the vicar-general not to have felt uneasy, for it must be remembered that Spain had very recently unearthed a sect known as the *Alumbrados*. It was not very numerous and made up of foolish rather than malicious people, but Spain was proud of its orthodoxy and it was believed that there might be a similarity of doctrine, if not an organic connection, between the *Alumbrados* and the heretics appearing in Germany. It is not to be wondered at that Ignatius was briefly under a cloud. Rather than contend with the suspicion, Ignatius decided to leave.

At the University of Salamanca, where he was in attendance the following year, things were not much better for him. There he and his companions attracted the attention of the Inquisition, which was under the direction of the Dominicans. He was detained in prison for a time while inquiries were made into his activities. The Dominicans began by inviting Ignatius to a meal in their friary and were at first cordial on the surface, though afterward they were more severe than the authorities at Alcalá had been, for after dinner they placed him and several of his friends in prison for three weeks where they were kept chained to a stake while the investigation was under way.

The Dominicans, however, precisely because they were more thorough in their investigations than Figueroa, actually did Ignatius a useful service. They did not merely subject him to questioning about the doctrine he held regarding the Trinity and the Blessed Sacrament; they demanded to see the *Spiritual Exercises*. In this, the only point that troubled them was Loyola's discussion of the distinction between mortal and venial sin. This they fastened upon, not because it contained doctrinal error, but because they questioned why a man who had had no theological training had ventured to express opinions about such matters. To this Ignatius replied calmly, "Decide whether what I have said is true or not. If it is not true, then condemn it." The questioners, not very fairly, would decide nothing, though it is obvious that if heresy had been found a condemnation would have been quickly forthcoming. Instead they sent Ignatius and the friends arrested with him back to their cell.

In the end the judges, having discussed the questions involved among themselves, did no more than issue an order that this distinction must not be talked about at large until Ignatius and his companions had studied for four more years, with which they released them. It was a verdict that was inconclusive but not altogether unreasonable, for while the written text presented to the Dominicans contained nothing to which positive exception could be taken, there was no telling into what errors at some future date an untrained man might not fall, perhaps completely inadvertently. The Inquisitors expressed a high opinion of Ignatius but insisted that he do as they commanded. Nevertheless theological enemies had been made, and though the most violent of these, the celebrated theologian Melchior Cano, does not seem to have had anything whatever to do with this incident, he must have heard about it from his Dominican confrères. If so, it is not unlikely that a grain of suspicion was sown in his mind and was the beginning of his subsequent animosity. It no doubt also went against Ignatius that before this the authorities at Alcalá had been uneasy.

At Salamanca Ignatius may have had little groups of pious persons who liked to talk with him about divine things, but now he was more cautious than he had been at Alcalá, or he had begun to have a clearer concept as to what was in store for him; he began to think of going elsewhere with his companions. At the University there were several men who went on from there, as Ignatius himself did, to Paris, and they were later to be among the first band of Jesuits, but at this time Ignatius does not seem to have encountered them, Salamanca being a large town and the stay of Ignatius brief. His followers in Salamanca were three men named Arteaga, Cacéres and Sa. They intended to join him in Paris, but various circumstances prevented this. One of the three joined another religious order, the two others became priests; so all may be said to have been influenced by Ignatius Loyola, even though they did not finally go so far as to throw in their lot with him. After all, this is scarcely to be wondered at, as Ignatius as yet had no more definite plan to propose than that they would do well, as friends, to keep together: the project of the Company of Jesus did not come into being for another fifteen years.

But by now Ignatius had made up his mind not to remain in Spain, where probably he would have continued to meet obstacles and where, by employing hindsight we can see that he would not have been able to work to the best advantage. Therefore he picked the greatest of all universities, that of Paris. So after a short visit to Barcelona and the women who had befriended him — it was from these that he had obtained the bill of exchange for twenty-five crowns which was his total fortune — he set out on foot, limping toward the north. What few belongings he had, he packed upon a *burro;* they probably did not consist of more than a second outfit of clothing about as shabby as what he had on, a few books and lecture notes, and the manuscript of the *Spiritual Exercises.*

Five

Paris

From barcelona Ignatius could take the easy way north that avoids the craggier Pyrenees. At this time France and Spain were again at war, and there were stories of atrocities, such as the burning alive by the French of the Spaniards they captured, that might have given Ignatius pause had he listened to his friends. However, in his poor garb and alone except for his little donkey loaded with books, he pressed on; and the road that he followed from the east coast of Spain seems to have presented no difficulties. Only a few days later he reached Toulouse, and though there were still many weary miles to Paris, they all stretched through flat or only gently rolling country.

He had not spent much time while on this journey at Barcelona, and there he delayed only so long as was needed to pay some courtesy calls, and possibly went there partly because he guessed that he would never have the chance to see old friends again. But in Paris he was to spend seven years, by far the longest stretch of his life in one place since he had left Loyola Castle during adolescence, and until he went to Rome. It was in Paris at the University that he found all his permanent disciples, the whole group, with one exception (the Savoyard, Blessed

Peter Faber), men from the Iberian peninsula. Francis
Xavier was a Basque like himself; another was a Portuguese, Simon Rodriguez; still another, Laynez, was one
who had like many Spaniards a strong infusion of Jewish
blood, as may also have been the case with the somewhat consequential Nicholas Bobadilla.

At first Ignatius enrolled at the Collège de Montaigu,
which was midway between the Porte Saint Jacques and
the Porte Saint Marceau on the hill of Saint Genevieve
and not far from the wall of the city. It had had among
its recent students Jean Calvin, still ostensibly orthodox,
but he probably left the place at just about the time that
Loyola arrived. One is obliged to say "probably," because
though Ignatius would not have been likely to mention
him, Calvin otherwise would certainly have indicated
that Ignatius was an old acquaintance when he was later
making the highly uncomplimentary references that he
did to the Jesuits. Erasmus and Rabelais were also alumni
of this college and neither had much good to say of it
(though it enjoyed a high reputation), but this was
mainly because of the poor food and wine provided.
Erasmus had, as we know from other grumblings of his,
a delicate stomach; we know, too, that it is a tradition at
almost every school and college — right to our own day
— to complain about the fare. In truth this is often not
very good, but it is rarely as bad as we are asked to believe.

There were several classifications of students, for nobody was debarred for lack of means. There was, to
begin with, the *cameristes* and *portionistes*, who paid
their own expenses in full. Then there were the *bursars*,
or as we should say, the scholarship men. Finally
there were the *martinets*, something like those students

who work their way through college in the United States. As they usually did not get much free time for classes, they often remained until they were quite grizzled, and then left without taking a degree. But the majority left after a month or two—whence their name of "birds of passage." Such students were there mainly because membership of the university conferred certain privileges and not because they expected to put their studies to much, if any, use. Ignatius was hardly brilliant enough to win a scholarship, and he was not able to find work as a *martinet* or as a servant to one of the Montaigu masters, no one being willing to hire a middle-aged cripple such as he. The twenty-five crowns he had brought with him from Barcelona was stolen, and he was soon destitute, forced to depend for subsistence on the alms he begged on the streets.

Despite his hard life Ignatius remained at the Montaigu for a year and a half, until he had acquired all that he could there in the way of a foundation for his Latin study. On the other side of the narrow alley stood a newer, cleaner and more progressive institution, the Collège de Sainte-Barbe. It had been founded about sixty years earlier by Geoffrey Lenormant, who possibly chose the name by intertwining his devotion to St. Barbara with a reminder of five mnemonic lines of Latin verse which are intended as a clue to the nineteen modes of the syllogism. The first of these is *Barbara, Celarent, Darii, Ferioque, Prioris,* which of course means nothing as it stands but is useful to a student who needs to have his memory jogged.

The rector of the college was a Diego Gouvea, and he had turned the establishment almost into a preserve for Portuguese students, he himself working under some kind

of a commission from King John III. But all the students
were not Portuguese or even Spaniards, by any means,
and Ignatius went there because he was able to share a
room with Francis Xavier and the Savoyard Peter Faber.

The main attraction for Ignatius, some say, was his
fellow Basque, Xavier, a much more advanced student,
who promised to give him some free tutoring. Of this the
brilliant Francis soon tired, but then the good-natured
Peter Faber came forward. He had started his studies
at the same time as Francis and, the son of a shepherd on
the Alpine slopes, he had about him a natural sunny
goodness. That is perhaps a still more remarkable fact to
record than that, while still a boy, Peter had taken a
private vow of chastity. That he was a man of ability
emerges from his later history; under him Ignatius, who
was still backward, must have made something like the
kind of progress that he had made under the private tui-
tion of Ardeval during 1524–26. Really Ignatius stood in
some need of help in his studies. Peter Faber, the student
who gave the tutoring, younger but more advanced than
Ignatius, had a genius for friendship.

Like all the Paris colleges of the time, the fare at the
Collège de Sainte-Barbe was meager and the living quarters uncomfortable. The three men in the room to which
Ignatius moved exemplify the democracy that prevailed
in the universities of that day. They were two Basque
hidalgos and a peasant boy from Savoy. The colleges
of that time were subjected in some respects to a severity
of discipline (which went side by side with much laxity)
that would today not be tolerated. It seems that on a
certain occasion Ignatius Loyola, on one of his errands
of charity, made visits to quarters from which he might
easily have brought back a serious epidemic to the whole

college. Gouvea felt that this should not go unpunished,
nor was an ordinary birching considered sufficient. Ignatius was accordingly sentenced to run the gauntlet
after dinner, and everybody there took off his belt or provided himself with a piece of knotted cord for the occasion. The students were, however, at the last moment
deprived of the chance of using their scourges, for just at
the moment when everybody stood ready to take part
in the punishment, the rector entered the dining-room
with Ignatius walking most amicably by his side. Satisfactory explanations had been made and the running of
the gauntlet had been called off.

It is likely that Ignatius paid Peter Faber something
for his tutoring, and it is even possible that Francis
Xavier, when short of money, did not disdain borrowing
from one who was as good a gentleman as himself. This
much is certain: Ignatius, discouraged at his small success in begging alms in Paris, decided to make during
vacations begging trips to the Low Countries and even
to England. As his personal needs were small, and his
charm great, he obtained more money than he needed
and used it to help poor students. One should not forget
the businesslike way in which he handled this money.
Ordinarily he did not hand out donations, but rather
loans that were to be repaid. The money he obtained was
not taken in the form of cash but was sent to him —
whether from Flanders or England or Spain — in the
form of a letter of exchange drawn upon a Paris mer-
chant. In short, Ignatius established what amounted to
a small bank, but took no part in its operations, no doubt
because he preferred to remain personally poor.

On one of his begging trips to Bruges, Loyola made
the acquaintance of Juan Luis Vivès, the celebrated

humanist, who had been a close friend of Chancellor
More's in Chelsea. In fact, it was More who had induced
Vivès to go to England, where he had drawn up a plan
of studies for the use of the future Queen Mary. As More
was not clapped into the Tower until 1534, it may well
have been that Vivès gave Ignatius a letter of introduction to that open-handed man. But whether it was from
Sir (now Saint) Thomas More or from some of the
wealthy Spanish merchants in London and in the Low
Countries, Ignatius was kept supplied with what he
needed at the University.

A point that can be only conjectural is that the *Ratio
Studiorum*, a scheme of studies later adopted by the
Jesuits, derived something from Vivès. But we must remember that the *Ratio* was not issued in the time of
Ignatius — though it was a codification of his educational
ideas — but in that of his fourth successor, Acquaviva.
Moreover, the *Ratio* to an even greater extent (and by
definite declaration) modeled itself upon the methods
used at the University of Paris. The most accurate word
to say here is that the *Ratio Studiorum* freely took its
good where it could find it and represents an amalgam of
the best educational theories then current. But Ignatius
picked up a good deal from his discussions with Vivès,
as he may also have done from Sir Thomas More, whose
learned household has been described as a "domestic university." These two men were in several respects fore-
runners of Jesuit educational methods, however much
the *Ratio* may have modified and improved upon their
ideas.

Though at Paris, as at Salamanca, several of the men
whom Ignatius attracted dropped off after a while, others
among his slowly gathered disciples remained firm. Two

of them — Laynez and Salmeron, who were to win such distinction at the Council of Trent — had casually encountered Loyola as early as the days at Alcalá. Then there was Bobadilla who had studied philosophy and theology at both Valladolid and Alcalá. As they were all doing what we should call postgraduate work at Paris, it is a wonder that they were not already priests, unless the explanation is that they were still uncertain what they were going to do with their lives and, as this was the humanistic age, had taken all knowledge for their province. We can find a striking illustration of this mode of procedure in the case of the English Reginald Pole. He was at this time thirty or so, and he had known from the outset that he was going to follow an ecclesiastical career, but in the meanwhile he gave himself over to the delights of pure scholarship. Much against his will, he had been made a cardinal in 1537, narrowly escaping a dozen years later election to the Papacy (though still only a deacon). He was not ordained priest until 1557, when he also accepted the archbishopric of Canterbury under Queen Mary. Earlier in his career he had been suggested as a suitable husband for his cousin, the Queen of England, until, most unfortunately, she married Philip of Spain. Under somewhat similar (though not such magnificent) circumstances the best prepared of the disciples of Ignatius wished to remain at the University, as ordination to the priesthood would oblige them to accept a benefice; therefore they deferred it indefinitely.

The disciple that Ignatius found by far the hardest to win was the *hidalgo* Francis Xavier. This was probably because Francis had long had his eye on a canonry in Pamplona Cathedral, which would have been a very comfortable appointment. The Xavier family had hitherto neglected to secure for him the certification that he came, on both his father's and his mother's side and for a long way back, of stock which while perhaps not of the highest nobility was yet unstained by any illegitimacy or even any tincture of Jewish blood. In Spain they were very particular about such matters, and nowhere more so than in the Basque country. The canons of Pamplona did not propose electing anybody to their closed corporation unless he could prove that he was unimpeachably of the gentry. Until a vacancy occurred there was no use in the Xavier family's pressing Francis' name. One would gather from the fact that Loyola's priest-brother took a mistress (or "uncanonical wife" as it was called) that the canons of Pamplona would not have been terribly shocked had Francis Xavier done much the same after he had become a canon, so long as he carried out his not very onerous duties and avoided giving notorious scandal.

One is reminded of what Edward Gibbon — very briefly a convert to Catholicism during adolescence — wrote of the Anglican Establishment in his *Autobiography*. There he used the amusing phrase "the fat slumbers of the Church." Spain of course contained a number of most zealous and devoted priests. But most of these were found in one or other of the reformed religious orders; the average parish priest was usually only a respectable person, and not one of those whom the zeal of the Lord has eaten up.

When at last a vacancy at Pamplona occurred, the Xavier family presented the certificate of Francis' high breeding. But when he learned that the long desired canonry was his for the taking, he had completely changed his point of view and was consumed with apostolic fervor. The reason was that he was now converted, and though he postponed making the Spiritual Exercises under Ignatius, as had most of the other disciples in a group, he was already inflamed by the Ignatian ideal and way of life.

We know that up to this point Xavier had kept himself quite clear of the dissolute courses into which one of the professors was more than ready to initiate him, yet he had conveyed the impression of being a rather worldly young man. But there was nothing worse to be said against him than that he wore fashionable clothes and maintained a servant and a horse and was always ready to engage in the rough-and-tumble sports (which usually ended in a most enjoyable free-for-all fight) in vogue among the students. It is possible that he looked upon himself with some complacency, for though his virtue may have largely reposed upon fastidiousness, at least he had shown himself a good deal more virtuous than many of those around him.

One would infer, too, that he now and then spoke to Ignatius of his expectation of obtaining a canonry at Pamplona, of what a fine, fat living that would be, and perhaps had hinted, broadly enough, that with his family connections, he might eventually obtain still higher office in the Church. He may be pardoned for thinking that such a life as he proposed was in no way reprehensible, though one of his generous nature probably divined that it left something to be desired. This may have been why Ignatius is said to have asked him, "What shall it profit a man if he gain the whole world and lose his own soul?" If at first this was a little irritating to Francis, he was not long in getting Loyola's point.

André Bellesort, the author of a brilliant little life in French of Xavier, suggests that Francis, instead of trying to meet an argument that was, after all, unanswerable, was in the end won by the Ignatian psychology. It was no good to reply that even a well-beneficed ecclesiastic might save his soul; the trouble, Bellesort suggests, was not that Francis had too much ambition, but that he did not have ambition enough. What were comfortable canonries compared with the glorious, if very arduous, work which Ignatius envisioned Xavier's doing for God?

There were, however, several factors operating in the opposite direction, in which we may be sure that Francis felt that he owed something to his family who had supported him — and in some "style" — while he was at the University: they naturally felt, in view of all the money they had spent, especially as they were hardly rich, that Francis should take advantage of opportunities that came his way. Ignatius later confessed that of all the men he had set out to win Francis Xavier was the most obdurate. He, too, being a Basque, had iron in his soul, even if it was mixed with some mercury in his case. If Ignatius persisted, this was because of his insight. The stone that accepts the chisel with most difficulty is the stone that keeps the eventual inscription most firmly. The two big volumes that contain the material gathered during the process for the canonization of Xavier is prefaced by a Latin distich which I will venture to render roughly as:

> *Of Xavier many miracles we hear;*
> *Ignatius did one greater — Xavier.*

All the disciples gathered at Paris were remarkable men, the only ones about whom the world learned next to nothing being the few who dropped away. But of all the band there was none more outstanding than the fashion-

able, engaging, easy-going Basque *hidalgo*. His conversion was obtained in the spring of 1533, so that Francis
was at Ignatius' side before Salmeron, Laynez and Bobadilla. These four with Faber and Rodriguez made up Loyola's original group. Toward them Ignatius was in the
position not of a superior but of an elder brother, with a
vote in their consultations no weightier than theirs.

With them, there was no formal plan; they only desired to work for the greater glory of God and as a little
band of brothers. Like Ignatius, they wished after becoming priests to go as pilgrims to Jerusalem — this time
together — and there to decide whether their future lay
in converting the Turks, or in other lands to which they
might be sent by the Pope. They also decided to bind
themselves by vows of poverty and chastity.

On August 15th of that year, the feast of the Assumption of Our Lady and the anniversary of Loyola's conversion in 1521, the whole group of seven friends assembled by agreement and in a body crossed to the other
side of the river. Above them rose the hill of Montmartre,
where a little chapel, not in good repair, belonging to
some Benedictine nuns had been placed at their disposal.
They were told that they might use the crypt, perhaps
because it was the only part of the building that was
usable. There Peter Faber, the only priest as yet among
them, said Mass and administered Holy Communion. As
he distributed the Sacrament he paused before every
man, with the Host in his hand, and each man in this
way made his vows. Instead of making that of obedience
every man vowed to go to the Holy Land, not realizing
that this was something that was to prove impossible.

August 15, 1534, has some claim to be considered as
the date of the origin of the Company of Jesus, though

it did not formally come into being until six years later. It is clear from statements subsequently made by some of the men present at Montmartre that there was no idea as yet of the founding of a religious order. If Ignatius had so much as thought of this as an eventual possibility, it must have been very vaguely; he never spoke of anything so nebulous to his friends.

Six

Italy

AFTER THE CEREMONY on Montmartre the seven brethren continued to live apart from one another, bound only by the community of their vow, by frequent visits, and a simple rule of life that consisted of daily meditation, examination of conscience twice a day, and weekly confession and Communion. And of course by now they all made the Spiritual Exercises.

The previous Easter, Ignatius had graduated as a master of arts of Paris, ahead of his younger and more brilliant companions. He had also entered on the study of theology with the Dominicans of the rue Saint-Jacques and in this his disciples followed him, continuing at the same time their course of studies for the master's degree at the University of Paris. In the spring of 1535, after eighteen months of theological study and as the result of long years of self-imposed austerity and privation, Ignatius' health broke down, and he was ordered by his doctors to leave Paris and return to his "native air." This he was willing to do, as it had been agreed by his companions that upon the completion of their studies they would join him in Venice where they hoped to embark upon their voyage to the Holy Land, and Loyola wished first to visit his family in Spain, probably feeling in his blood that he would never see them again. From Loyola

Castle he could take the road to Barcelona, and from there sail to Italy.

A word might be said of this visit to Spain. Azpeitia is about 550 miles from Paris, and when Ignatius entered the province of Guipúzcoa, he left the main road and took to mountain trails, as he intended to lodge at the hospital or hospice for travellers instead of enjoying the mild splendors of Loyola Castle. It was in all in vain; at Bayonne he was recognized by a man who hurried to the Castle with the news. But though the eldest of the Loyola brothers, suspecting his intentions and knowing how stubborn Ignatius could be, sent priests to bring him home, it was to the hospital of Azpeitia, just outside the Loyola domain, that he insisted on going after a journey that had taken a month.

It was at the hospital that he stayed, dressed like a penitent in gray serge and sandals, living the life of the poor, begging his own bread, wearing, it was discovered, a hair shirt and a chain around his waist, but caring for the wants of others, catechizing children and preaching to crowds to whom a great gentleman living as he did was a sensation. There were some quarrels that he patched up, but he was shocked to observe that some young women wore their hair as though they were married, though they were the concubines of priests, one of whom was a brother of Ignatius. Evidently this state of affairs deeply scandalized a man like Ignatius.

There is no space available to describe the visit home in greater detail. It is enough to say that worn out by his labors, which effected a number of conversions, Ignatius again fell ill, and not until July, 1535, was he able to leave for Valencia by a roundabout way that took him, always on foot, half over Spain since he wished to visit the families of the disciples he had left in Paris. At Valencia he boarded a ship bound for Genoa, and after divers adventures arrived in Venice in the last days of 1535. Here he was to wait a whole year for his companions, a time spent in giving the Spiritual Exercises to those who sought him out, and in the study of theology.

Because of the outbreak of a new war between the Empire and France, there was bad feeling towards Spaniards. Therefore the group Ignatius had left in Paris had to alter the route they had intended to follow in joining him. Instead of striking for Italy through the south of France, they thought it safer to go through Lorraine, and then cross southern Germany on the way to Venice. They were obliged to practice a mild form of "Jesuitism," for when they ran into a band of soldiers, the Frenchmen among them called out that they were Frenchmen, or the Spaniards that they were Spaniards, and that they were on a pilgrimage to the shrine at Loreto. This famous shrine was on the Adriatic, and nearer Rome than Venice, but they did have a hope of being able to visit it. The company of course went on foot, carrying in addition to a second pilgrim's robe only a breviary, a Bible, and such manuscript notes as they could not leave behind, all stuffed into a leather knapsack. The whole group at last came together in Venice on January 8, 1537.

They had intended to sail for the Holy Land at once, but Ignatius thought they should first go to Rome to ask the blessing of the Pope, Paul III. Almost immediately afterward he got it into his head that the Emperor's ambassador to the Holy See, Dr. Pedro Ortiz, had a personal animosity against him, and so decided to remain in Venice while the others went on to Rome.

This was a strange idea on the part of Ignatius, but he

had brought himself to believe that it was Dr. Ortiz who had let it be known in Paris that he had been under suspicion of the ecclesiastical authorities at both Alcalá and Salamanca. Dr. Ortiz may, indeed, have mentioned this as a bit of amusing gossip, but he was in fact well disposed, as we shall soon see. Ignatius was not without reason in fearing that similar reports, if set in circulation in Rome, might be damaging, and so preferred to keep out of sight.

As things turned out, it was Ortiz himself who introduced the group of friends from the University of Paris to the Pope, and was to prove a steadfast friend. He had been sent to Rome to look after the interests of the Emperor's aunt, Katherine of Aragon, and he had remained there after her death in 1536 because Anne Boleyn, the famous trouble-maker in England, had been executed the same year; the situation in England was such that the diplomatic skill of a man conversant with the whole story seemed more than ever desirable. It must not be forgotten that with Anne Boleyn out of the way high hopes were for a time entertained that Henry VIII would close his quarrel with the Papacy — something that several times appeared likely to happen.

The Pope, when told by the Companions of their plan to go to the Holy Land, commended the idea as good in itself but added that he did not think they would go; he had private information that war between Venice and the Turks was on the point of breaking out. He was, however, so taken with these graduates of the University of Paris that he invited them to stage a debate for his edification while he ate his dinner. Debates of this sort were, at that time, a favorite diversion, but more than that was involved in this case.

When the Pope learned that only Peter Faber was a priest, he signed a document empowering any bishop to whom it was presented to ordain the other Companions without further delay, for he saw from their debate that they were all well prepared. Though little time was lost on their return to Venice in obtaining ordination to the priesthood, all went into a lengthy period of retreat before saying their first Masses.

A few months later the war between Venice and the Turks had become a reality, and the Companions, who had separated in groups of twos for the retreat following their ordination, reassembled at Vicenza where they lived in community and where they resumed their austerities and preaching. As the winter approached they were forced to come to some decision: since the opportunity to fulfill their vow to visit Palestine was remote they must draw up a future plan of action. It was decided that Ignatius, Faber and Laynez would go to Rome and place themselves at the Pope's disposal while the others would disperse, again in pairs, to preach and hear confessions and to recruit new members for their band.

Before they dispersed the question was brought up of what they should answer in case someone asked who they were. In Paris they had been called *Iniguistas,* from the Spanish name of their leader, but now "they began to pray and think," writes Polanco, "what title would best suit them, and considering that over them they had no head but Jesus Christ, it seemed right that they should adopt the Name of Him who was their head and that they should be called the Company of Jesus."

But even with this name chosen it was some time before the Companions so much as thought of forming themselves into a religious order, for while such an idea may have flickered through the mind of this or that man among them, each treated it as fanciful, so that we do not know who first ventured to express it. When it came into being it burst into flame, as the result of a chance remark of Pope Paul III when all of them were in Rome. As we have seen, after the members of the group had been ordained priests, they went out in pairs preaching or cate-chizing. They made a special point of giving their services in the not very efficiently conducted hospitals of the time. When they did so, they shrank from no kind of work, however menial or disgusting it was. They were but marking time but, in doing so, preparing themselves for the great works — often of a completely different kind — they were soon to undertake.

One thing should be carefully noted about these cou-ples on their little tours. Though they had no superior as yet, Ignatius had always enjoyed a moral ascendency among them, so that his suggestions had the force of directives. He proposed that, for the sake of good order, even of two men, one should be considered in charge; so each of the two took it in weekly turns to act as superior. The arrangement was eminently sensible and reminds one of how St. Francis of Assisi sometimes al-lowed groups of four to go into periods of retirement for the sake of spiritual refreshment. In their case two of the men should be styled "mothers" for a week, and the other two "sons," with a reversal of the position the next week. The purpose was that the "sons" should be set com-pletely free for contemplation while the "mothers" at-tended to whatever domestic duties needed to be done. Ignatius may never have heard of St. Francis' plan and have devised the simpler concept himself. However this may be, the scheme was based upon commonsense. With regard to Ignatius, it emphasized the fact that the group had no superior, and though it must have entered his head that, when one was eventually elected, the lot would fall on him, he was hoping against hope that he would be able to refuse so decisively that somebody else would be chosen. In all of which one cannot fail to see inevitability.

In Rome Ignatius and his two companions met at first with a modest success; many prominent personages came to them to make the Spiritual Exercises, additions were made to their numbers, and in the spring of 1538 Ignatius was able to reunite his scattered brethren at their first home in Rome, a little cottage near the Trinità dei Monti. That May they moved to larger but still humble quarters in the center of the city and were authorized to preach in various churches and squares in Rome, to administer the sacraments, and to give instructions in Christian doctrine.

At about this time Dr. Ortiz, whom Ignatius had earlier feared would prove an enemy, went so far as to apply for admission to this group. Ignatius took him seriously enough to go with him to the Benedictine Abbey of Monte Cassino to give him the Spiritual Exercises in full (something that occupied a whole month) by way of preparation. Several stories have come down to us about this, stories which were no doubt substantially true but which, one suspects, have been humorously embellished. The commonly accepted version of the matter is that Ortiz was finally refused as one of the Companions because he was too fat. Obviously there was more to it than that, but it was probably true that the corpulence of Dr. Ortiz — coupled to the fact that he was getting on in years — sometimes made him drowsy.

We hear that on one occasion Ignatius had to execute a
Basque dance to revive the man's attention. What never
seems to be allowed for is that the taking of the Exercises
in full was an ordeal for Ortiz, whose piety had been
nourished from sources of another character, and was a
bit too much for a middle-aged man who had a burden
of flesh to carry around. There is another reason that
should be mentioned. Dr. Ortiz was the Emperor's ambassador to the Holy See, and as has been said, had gone
to Rome to look after the affairs of Katherine of Aragon.
Had Ortiz been an ordinary ambassador it may be that
his age and corpulence and somnolence would have been
overlooked, but there were sound reasons for thinking
that he might be of much more service to the Church by
going on as before than by joining the Companions. So
far from holding any grudge against them, his relations
remained as cordial as ever. It is more than possible that,
upon thinking things over, he fully accepted the opinion
of Ignatius and came to see that he was best employed
in the service of Charles V.

If Ortiz had shown himself a friend rather than an
enemy in Rome, an unfriendly critic and a positive enemy
were not long in appearing. An Augustinian imagined
that he had discovered heresy in the Companions' doctrine
and so started preaching against them. He was silenced
only after much difficulty, for he enlisted the aid of a
servant Xavier had had in Paris and who had followed
them to Rome. Earlier, some say, this man had tried to
murder his master (more likely he had intended to give
him only an incapacitating wound, so as to prevent
Francis from throwing in his lot with Ignatius). This time
he actually asked to be admitted into the Company, and
when his application was refused he attempted to get

revenge through calumny. Ignatius who was sensitive to any malicious criticism that might be taken seriously enough to prevent his doing his work, demanded an investigation from the highest authority with the result that the man, named as Miguel Landivar, was run out of the city, and the Augustinian preacher was also banished by the governor of Rome.

At this point it may be remarked that sensitiveness to criticism — whether of the group or the Spiritual Exercises — did not reveal any special touchiness on the part of Ignatius, for at this stage criticism might prove to be very damaging. And Miguel knew enough about the Companions to give some plausibility to his attack, however unjustified.

We might introduce at this point another of those who stood aloof from Ignatius: the young layman (as he was then), St. Philip Neri. He was never opposed to the Jesuits, even if his relations with them were not so cordially intimate as those he later established with the Dominicans and Franciscans. Ignatius looked upon him almost as a son and unavailingly threw out hints several times that he would be glad to obtain his adhesion. The engaging and eccentric Philip, however, though he was totally unaware that it was to be his destiny in later life (when he *did* become a priest at last) to charm many of the members of the Roman Curia into conversion, was at least sure that he had no vocation to be a Jesuit. When Ignatius first knew him, though he was only a layman, Philip was sending a number of his disciples into religious orders. Loyola's humorous lament was, "Philip is like the bell on a church belfry, calling people to church but never getting inside the church himself." Philip used to laugh at this but knew what he was up to: it was not to be a Jesuit, though just what his life work was to be he did not then guess.

When in 1539 at last it was decided to ask the Pope's permission to found a new order, at once serious difficulties arose, difficulties which the Companions may have expected, or which could have been no great surprise to them. Many of the cardinals disapproved of the whole idea of new orders, and for a number of reasons. To begin with, the multiplication of religious institutes created administrative problems. Then the three groups of those classified as clerks-regular founded a short time before had not always made themselves very popular. Thus the Theatines, under the joint control of the gentle Cajetan and the irascible Caraffa, Bishop of Chieti, who not long afterward became Pope Paul IV, were so very strait-laced that people had begun to use "Theatine" and "hypocrite" as almost interchangeable terms.

Furthermore, the Capuchin reform of the Franciscans, which occurred in 1525, had at its head at this time Bernardino Ochino, a popular preacher whose ideas were already suspected of having a Lutheran tinge, but who did not openly pass over to the Reform until 1542. A section of the Curia went so far as to argue, as we have seen earlier, that it would be better to suppress all orders except the Benedictines, the Franciscans and the Dominicans, which was certainly a drastic line to take. Had it prevailed it would have swept away the Carthusians, the only order which never needed to be reformed because it had never been deformed, the Carmelites, the Augustinians, the Brigittines, the Praemonstratensians, and the Gilbertines (the only religious order to be founded by an Englishman), as well as the recently established clerks-regular. More to the point here, this argument

would have prevented the Company of Jesus from coming into being.

Moreover such objectives can hardly be said to have
been new. When Francis of Assisi went before Innocent III in 1215 he was given permission to model the life
of the Friars Minor upon the Gospels (which could hardly
be refused) and to preach so long as the friars eschewed
theology and confined themselves to trying to bring people to repentance. Even that much served the purpose of
St. Francis, though the real Franciscan rule was not
formulated until several years later. However, when St.
Dominic presented himself before the Pope just a year
later with a definitely thought-out scheme in his head,
he was told that he would have to follow the existing
Rule of St. Augustine, the only feasible alternative being
the Rule of St. Benedict which would not have suited
him at all. Yet St. Augustine's regulations are hardly to
be called a rule and what controls Dominican life is
their *Constitutions*, a big volume constantly being enlarged or revised. But the so-called Rule of St. Augustine would have been of no use whatever to the Company
of Jesus, so radical was the departure they proposed to
make from all previous rules, though this is not to say that
their mode of life did not contain much that was in
perfect consonance with religious life as it had hitherto
been practiced.

Yet no written Constitutions were presented by them
for Papal approval, only a summary of what was in the
minds of the Companions, for even when the Constitutions were compiled by Ignatius they were quite brief,
and even so were not published until after the death of
the founder of the Jesuits. Nevertheless, Paul III accepted what was laid before him, though only tenta-

tively and with some restrictions in the Bull *Regimini militantis Ecclesiae,* issued on September 27, 1540. This was not so much a final papal approval of the Company of Jesus as permission to draw up their Constitutions; but what was given sufficed for the moment. Even that much could have been subsequently withdrawn by Paul III himself or one of his successors. This, however, did not occur, as the Jesuits lost no time in demonstrating their enormous value. The story, which may be quite true, is that the Pope exclaimed, "Here is the finger of God!" Not always (or even often) is one able to discern with any certainty the workings of Providence. But this seems to be a case when there need be no presumption in thinking the matter unmistakably plain.

Seven

The Instrument

At this point it becomes quite necessary to interrupt the narration of events with a consideration of two matters of a more abstract nature, for unless this is done the story of the Company of Jesus cannot be properly understood. Accordingly I pause to insert two chapters, one on the Spiritual Exercises and the other on the Jesuit Constitutions. As to this, however, I must remark that my friend Father Francis X. Talbot, in his article on the Society of Jesus in the current *Encyclopedia Britannica*, declares that the Exercises should be regarded as the Jesuit rule. That is perfectly true, if we are thinking of the formation of Jesuits and their manner of life, but the Exercises called for, and received, a more definite implementation in the Constitutions. Accordingly each will be considered separately.

The Exercises, in their rudimentary form, were conceived as a mode of spiritual discipline for Ignatius Loyola himself, in the cave of Manresa in 1522, which was just after his conversion. They underwent revision for another twenty years before Ignatius was satisfied with them, but long before that he had brought them near enough to what he had in mind to use them with immense effect in the formation of his disciples; they were to be of all his many activities his main instrument,

at least for the making of Jesuits. Perhaps the educational
work of the Society became its most valuable undertaking, so far as the world at large is concerned, more
valuable, it may be argued, than even its missionary
enterprises, but these would have lost most of their
effect had they not been carried out by men whose
inner life was fashioned by the Exercises.

As everything began at Manresa it might be as well
to ask what, if any, are the derivations of the Spiritual
Exercises. As has been already said, an absolute originality is something that virtually never exists. To begin
with, Ignatius was drawing upon the common stock of
religious belief, but, apart from what this or that spiritual
writer may have written, Ignatius made his exposition
in a highly novel way. For instance, if there are any
echoes of St. Bernard, they are faint, and Ignatius at
Manresa (1522–23) is most unlikely to have read St.
Bernard — though he may have done so during his
student days in Paris.

It is not to be denied that at Manresa Ignatius had as
his confessor a Benedictine named Juan Chanones who,
after having been a secular priest, turned monk in his
early thirties, in the year 1512.[1] This in itself would not
be much to build upon were it not for the fact that the
most famous of the abbots of his community was Francisco García de Cisneros, who wrote a book entitled
Ejercitatorio de la vida espiritual which it may be pre-
sumed was loaned to Ignatius by Chanones. But even
this cannot be decisively proved, and even if it could,
would not suffice to show a Benedictine origin. It is, however, likely enough that Ignatius was deeply impressed

[1] He long outlived Ignatius, dying in 1569, and has been beatified.

by the work of Cisneros, so that there is undoubtedly a sense in which the Benedictines contributed to his spiritual development. But the similarities between the Exercises and the *Ejercitatorio* do not extend beyond about twenty formulas, such as might be used by any writer on spiritual subjects. Père Dudon says emphatically of Cisneros' work: "There could not be less resemblance to the work of Ignatius of Loyola. There are as many things that indicate notations made from Ludolph of Saxony or from Thomas à Kempis." In any case such details were not brought in as quotations but as things that Ignatius had made his own by constant brooding upon them. For example, the kind of imagery we find of a spiritual combat, might just as well be taken to demonstrate that John Bunyan was drawing upon Ignatius when he composed his *Holy War*.

The claims that have sometimes been put in by Dominicans or Franciscans to the effect that Ignatius drew upon the writings of members of their orders are still less substantial. There is only this to be said: the Dominicans had a friary at Montserrat and Ignatius had contacts with them. What has to be established is some kind of textual similarities; these may be explained by saying that remote similarities of this sort are not hard to discover, but they prove nothing definite. What may be said is that, while the mind of Ignatius may not have been luminously incandescent, he must have been much more clever than is usually supposed in covering up his tracks. The truth seems to be that Ignatius took his good wherever he could find it, but so far from being a copier or adapter of previous writers, he produced in the Exercises something which, if not as completely original as we are sometimes invited to believe, was yet one of the world's most formative books — that is, if it be called a book as we ordinarily understand the word.

In short, those who have been intent in digging up sources, have not succeeded in unearthing anything worth mentioning. The mind of Ignatius, we may be sure, received a kindling and sharpening from what he read, but his manner of presenting it is highly novel, whether or not it is the manner that makes the greatest appeal to all people. We have here an illustration of the truth that it is much better to digest a few — even a very few — books thoroughly than to run rapidly through a great many, as this kind of reading rarely leaves much impression. It was greatly to the advantage of Ignatius Loyola that he was never a bookworm, perhaps even that he did not seriously set about getting an education until he was over thirty. Though his brains by that time were less nimble than a boy's, maturity had given him a knowledge of himself and of his fellows. Yet in the last analysis we are obliged to say of him that he was a genius, and if he does not correspond very closely to the pictures that most men form of a genius — so much the better for him.

When we come to a consideration of the *Spiritual Exercises* we must bear in mind that in 1522–23, when Ignatius composed the first draft, he was totally unacquainted with the two greatest of the modern exponents of mysticism, St. Teresa and St. John of the Cross, who were both alive but at that time were only children. The general scheme which they accepted and upon which they elaborated with such insight and literary skill had, however, long been known. This was the division of the spiritual life into three stages as made by that unidentified medieval writer who, in order to secure authority for his books, all of which have real value, palmed himself off on the world as the Dionysius mentioned by St. Paul.

These stages, which still are classical, are called the purgative, the illuminative, and the unitive way, and are very real, though it must not be forgotten that they are not three rungs in a ladder up which one climbs hand-over-fist, but which overlap, so that even the soul who has attained union with God may still stand in some need of purgation. At Montserrat Ignatius would have heard something about this, and the first three "weeks" of the Exercises more or less correspond to these three stages. Moreover, his Dominican friends at Montserrat, not to mention his Benedictine confessor, would undoubtedly have drawn his attention to the famous formula of St. Thomas Aquinas that the purpose of all who essayed the "mixed" life was *Tradere aliis contemplata*. What Ignatius attempted was something of the same sort: to deliver to others the fruits of contemplation, though this was something that came later, when he used the Exercises to aid others to attain perfection.

I think I might here quote something from an article written by Father Emerich Coreth in a German scholarly magazine and reprinted in part in our own *Theology Digest*. Father Emerich seems to me to put his finger upon Ignatius' solution by quoting Jerome Nadal, one of the two assistants given the Saint in his latter years, who distinguished the Jesuit aim from *Tradere aliis contemplata*, to which nevertheless it has a kinship. Nadal's formula is "the contemplative in action." Mary and Martha are still sisters, even if they now wear somewhat different dresses, but our Jesuit author, while insisting upon the indispensable need for prayer points out: "Ignatius no

longer places perfection in a contemplative element, not
even in religious contemplation, if by this is meant formal prayer, contemplation and other 'exercises,' but es-
sentially in the perfection of action which is undertaken
purely for the sake of God." To quote him again, he says:
"Work for the sanctification of others is not only the
highest fulfillment of the love of neighbor — because it
concerns itself with highest good attainable for another
— but it is also the highest fulfillment of the love of God,
in so far as all the toil and anxiety of work, even the re-
nunciation of contemplative quiet with God alone, is
undertaken for the love of God as a surrender of one's
self entirely to the plans and wishes of God in order to
work with Him in His redemptive mission in the world."

It is probably unnecessary for me to give any analysis
of the Spiritual Exercises, for anybody is free to read this
little work, though few people do so; indeed, many who
take up the volume in which they are contained are dis-
appointed, precisely because they treat it as an ordinary
book. It may be read through in an hour, but if it is regarded as a devotional work — that is, as a book — it is
almost certain to be regarded as dry and not very profitable spiritually. This is because it is almost as unemo-
tional as a treatise of geometry, its purpose being not to
pour information into a reader's mind but to serve as a
work of practical guidance for one wishing to make a retreat. The retreat master is even warned not to suggest
too much but to leave it to the exercitant to find out by
reflection what is of importance for his own spiritual life.
As Father Rickaby says, he is "to play the game himself,
not to be a mere looker-on or listener . . . he must sweat
and toil for himself, think hard and seek God fervently."

To describe the matter briefly and as an outsider who
is doing his best but who is painfully aware of how he

falls short, the main idea of the Exercises is to help the one making them to try to discover and to conform to the will of God in all things, and to give him the energy and courage to follow that will. With this aim in view he is guided through four periods or "weeks" of meditation. The first week is preliminary — a digging up of old roots and weeds for the sowing that is to be done later; its meditations are on sin and its consequences. In what follows Christ becomes the entire content of the Exercises; the meditations of the second week are on His life on earth, the third week on His Passion, the fourth on His risen life. A certain number of instructions are added to teach the exercitant how to pray, how to avoid scruples, how to think with the Church and — most important of all — how to follow a vocation in life without being swayed by love of self or of the world.

There is nothing startling in all this; the subjects of the meditations are commonplaces of spirituality. It is rather in the psychological insight with which they are given their logical connection that the effectiveness of the Exercises is to be found, and a paramount point is the extent to which they engender "self-activity."

How exceedingly laconic Ignatius often is appears in this meditation from the "Mysteries of the Life of Christ": On page 100 of the edition I am using, one reads:

Of the Mysteries from the Cross to the Sepulchre Inclusively
(St. John xix, 25–39)

1. He was taken down from the Cross by Joseph and Nicodemus in the presence of His sorrowful Mother.
2. His body was carried to the sepulchre, anointed, and buried.
3. Guards were set.

And that is all — mere points upon which the meditation
is to be made. The retreat-master is to fill in the rest, or
rather, to make suggestions to the retreatants who are
making the Exercises. While Ignatius at almost every turn
expects what he calls "the composition of place," or the
holding before one with all the force of the imagination
the scene upon which the meditation should be made, he
himself uses hardly any description. This is true even of
the famous — perhaps one might say the crucial — meditation known as "The Two Standards." We get nothing
of the sort of thing that makes Milton's *Paradise Lost*
so magnificent and occasionally, as in his account of the
war conducted in heaven between the forces of Lucifer
and St. Michael, so appallingly absurd. When Ignatius
does expand a bit more, as in what he says of the insid-
iousness of sin — likening the Devil to a woman who,
when quarrelling with a man, loses courage and takes
to flight when the man shows himself undaunted — he still
manages to compress what he has to say to a couple of
sentences. It is quite a long disquisition for him when he
writes:

[The Devil] also acts like a false lover, inasmuch as he
wishes to remain hidden and undiscovered; for as this false
man, speaking with an evil purpose, and paying court to the
daughter of some honest man, wishes his conversations and
insinuations to be kept secret, and on the contrary, is much
displeased when the daughter discovers to her father, or the
wife to her husband, his deceitful words and his depraved
intention, because he easily infers that he cannot succeed in
the designs he has conceived; in the same way, when the enemy of our human nature obtrudes on a just soul his wiles and
deceits, he wishes and desires that they be furtively received
and kept secret, but he is very displeased when they are discovered to a good confessor or some other spiritual person

who knows his frauds and malice, because he infers that he cannot succeed in the wicked design he had conceived, as his evident frauds are laid open.

It will be enough for most people that they resist the satanic wiles, yet nobody can be secure who does not say what Ignatius writes on the initial page of his "First Principle and Foundation," that is, immediately after what he calls the "Annotations" but which we might call the Introduction:

We should make ourselves indifferent to all created things, in so far as it is left to the liberty of our will to do so, and is not forbidden; in such sort that we do not for our part wish for health rather than sickness, for wealth rather than poverty, for honor rather than dishonor, for a long life rather than a short one; and so in all things, desiring and choosing only those which most lead us to the end for which we were created.

This may seem so lofty as to be an unattainable ideal but is, in fact, the only possible basis for a dedicated life. More explicitly still, this appears in Ignatius' famous *Suscipe:* "Take, O Lord, and receive all my liberty, my memory, my understanding, and all my will, all that I have and possess. Thou hast given it to me; to Thee, O Lord, I restore it: all is Thine, dispose of it according to Thy will. Give me Thy love and Thy grace, for this is enough for me." Only by total surrender to God can the soul be safe. The idea is not of course new: for many people its classic expression is in Dante's great line, "In His will is our peace."

The *Spiritual Exercises,* one of the most famous of all books, and perhaps after the Bible and the *Imitation* one of the most influential, is not a book at all, but stands quite unique. Its structural scheme leaves something to be desired (though I am not prepared to say just what this is), and it is almost totally devoid of literary grace. It is a kind of spiritual drill-manual, something to be used to give general direction to the man who is conducting the Exercises. But it has proved to have such value that it has set hearts on fire and played a large role in the formation of many saints.

Melchior Cano, perhaps the greatest of the Dominican theologians of Loyola's own time, rather strangely objected that the Exercises were "too mystical," which cannot but suggest that Cano was hard put to it to find a stone to throw against the Jesuits. But perhaps he simply did not understand the work, or would not bother to understand it, because it was not the kind of devotional work to which he was accustomed. To this one can only say that had it been what the Dominican was expecting, while it might have given edification to a small circle, we should not have heard of it today; it would have failed of its purpose. What Ignatius gave us was a series of meditations, in which thought follows link by link, but which makes no attempt to charm.

Ignatius composed it in the first place for use in his own spiritual development, only later finding how much it could accomplish for others. All his first disciples, and every Jesuit through over four centuries has been moulded by it, all of them making the Spiritual Exercises in their full form, for which a whole month is needed. Yet the usefulness of the work does not end quite there: it was never intended to be restricted to Jesuits, and Ignatius was well aware that many pious laymen would be unable to take a month off for a retreat. These he expressly provided for: if a man was too busy with his secular duties and yet was anxious to improve his spiritual state, he could be given the Exercises in an abbreviated form, and if he could not spare even so much as a week, there are few well disposed people (women as well as men) who could not arrange for a long week end. Then at least they would derive some profit for their souls.

That is why all over the world Jesuits have established retreat houses, where sometimes the workingmen of a particular parish could attend, or a group of lawyers or doctors, though those who do assemble are often a group gathered more or less at random. There are also retreat houses for women, and though I have naturally not been present, I believe I am right in saying that their retreats, whether or not they are under the direction of a Jesuit, are based upon the Spiritual Exercises. The same is true of the annual retreats made by the diocesan clergy. Other religious orders now also give retreats, into which they impart something of their own spirit — the Benedictines, for example, laying, as is only to be expected, more emphasis than the Jesuits do upon the liturgy — but all of them being to a large extent based upon what Ignatius began at Manresa. One may even find Ignatian touches in most parish missions, for these — to some extent at least — have to be considered as retreats for those who can only attend at morning and evening for a week. It is quite incalculable what has been accomplished, directly or indirectly, in full or in a condensed way by the Spiritual Exercises. The intention in all such cases is to bring each retreatant, after he faces the fact of sin, to the foot of the Cross, to the feet of Christ, bringing it home to each in such a way that each should cry — O astounding thought! — "That Life, Death and Resurrection were *for me*.":

Se nascens dedit socium
Convescens in edulium
Se moriens in pretium
Se regnans dat in praemium.

(At birth our Brother He became;
At meat Himself as food He gives;
To ransom us He died in shame;
As our reward in bliss He lives.)

This is a consideration not intended to be confined to Jesuits, or members of religious orders, or the secular clergy, but is offered to all Christians who wish to reach a higher state of perfection, such as may be consonant with the duties of life to which they are bound.

Eight

The Jesuit Constitutions

THE FIRST THING to bear in mind is that the Constitutions were never presented to Pope Paul III and never seen by him. What he gave in 1540 was a general approval of the intentions that had been reached as a body by the Companions, and his permission to write their Constitutions, with the understanding of course that these would follow the same lines of what he had been told they meant to do. Such approval was necessarily tentative, as it was of course quite possible that details would be introduced which he could not accept; or it could happen that by the time the Constitutions were formulated as a written code, he would be dead, and that there would be on the papal throne another Pontiff who was not so favorable. But though the Constitutions did not in fact appear until the time of the high-handed Paul IV, who did not relish the way that Ignatius several times stood out against him, the Constitutions nevertheless passed the Papal scrutiny, though even after that had happened Paul IV insisted — but only by word of mouth — that one of their most important provisions be discarded.

About this more will be said in a moment. It is enough to say now that after Paul III's bull of 1540, Ignatius was commissioned by the Companions to draw up the Con-

stitutions formally and in writing. It should be added that
he did not so much as start this piece of work until he had
thought about it for several years, and that at every stage
he was careful to ask the opinion of the other members
of his order. Even after the work was completed and before it was submitted for Papal approval it was given a
couple of years' trial, to discover if it was going to be perfectly satisfactory in every detail before the Jesuits themselves officially promulgated it in all the parts of the
world in which they had, by that time, begun their operations. Therefore the Constitutions, unlike the Spiritual Exercises, must be considered to some degree a corporate enterprise.

Nevertheless the rules governing the Company may be
considered as an implementation of the Exercises, even
though the earlier work was of a purely spiritual character, whereas the Constitutions indicated, as briefly as
possible, the regulations which were to govern the order.
Both documents were highly individual, and reveal the
mind of Ignatius.

We may take it as certain that Ignatius worked with
other rules before him and that he necessarily largely
based himself upon that drawn up by St. Benedict. Yet
in doing so, he clearly discarded a good deal. It may also
be that he drew upon St. Basil here, St. Augustine there,
and St. Francis at some other place; nor would he have
neglected to study the rules that had been recently produced by the new groups of clerks-regular. What finally
emerged was hardly a rule, in the sense in which the word
is commonly used, but rather a collection of principles;
in this respect Ignatius more nearly resembled Basil or
Augustine than Benedict. Without going further into this
matter, it should be said that what he and his friends pro-

duced contains several novel departures from religious life as it had hitherto been practiced. Nevertheless the story that some Jesuits of former days used to relate, that the only books used by Ignatius were the Bible and the Breviary, is on the face of it fantastic. Père Dudon, who is himself a Jesuit, has said quite bluntly: "This is a pious fiction belied by facts, and little in keeping with the character of the man." It helps hagiography a good deal to discard such nonsense.

Today probably most people think that the main work of the Jesuits is the running of colleges; this is only because a large number of colleges are under their direction, though not so many as in the eighteenth century. But it should be understood that no special activity is to be called the Jesuits' "main" work, as there is hardly any form of work that they do not undertake. While it is true that they are quite different from the various institutes of nursing brothers, they nevertheless maintain hospitals (staffed by Sisters) which are usually, if not invariably, connected with one of their medical schools. Indeed, if one is compelled to pick out some Jesuit activity as "primary" with them, it would be what they do in the field of foreign missions or in the apostolic mode in some of our great cities. Their object is always the saving of souls, by any means that seems to be most called for. In this their educational, like their other enterprises, are a means to an end rather than an end in themselves. The same thing is of course true of all Catholic activities, whatever may be the order concerned, but this is specially true of what the Jesuits essay in education.

Ignatius was soon obliged to establish colleges — or if you like, seminaries or houses of study — for the training of young Jesuits, but it was not long afterward that circumstances obliged him to admit "extern" students as well, something which may have been first suggested by Laynez but which Ignatius himself saw to be desirable. Though the first Jesuit scheme of studies known as the *Ratio Studiorum* was not to be drawn up until Ignatius had been dead for thirty years, this embodied — at any rate in germinal form — what Ignatius had held from the start.

The first pupils of the Jesuits, being poor, could afford no fees. But no fees were charged, even when well-to-do youths crowded into their colleges, because Ignatius, most of all wishing to preserve his poverty, would accept payment for none of the services he rendered. At the door of the first educational establishment he opened in Rome was a tablet inscribed: *Scuola di Grammatica, D'Humanitá e Dotterina Christiana, Gratis.* All these first schools were maintained on endowments provided by benefactors. But when such endowments in later times were unattainable, and expensive equipment and lay teachers supplemented what the Jesuits did for nothing, fees had to be charged, if schools were to be maintained at all.

We must also remember that though today in the United States the Jesuits have a number of colleges and also preparatory schools of a kind which in some instances cater to the well-to-do, who expect to be well housed and well fed, nevertheless many Jesuit parishes have free parochial schools attached to them. We see a rather amusing instance of what the first Jesuits thought about education in St. Francis Xavier. When he first went to India he hit upon the device of leading a crowd of native urchins to school, marching at their head ringing a bell. Also, in his first catechism in Tamil, doctrine was imparted by the learning of rhymed verses.[1] But Xavier was a man of infinite resource, a great experimentalist and innovator. The point to seize is that the realistic Jesuits refused to be too strictly tied down by hard-and-fast regulations, but held themselves ready to deal with any situation that arose. The Constitutions were flexible enough to cover later developments, which were of course inevitable.

Every religious order puts its novices through a novitiate. But where other orders consider a year of probation enough, the Jesuits insist on two. It is commonly said that they aim at efficiency; if so, it is an efficiency largely derived from the Spiritual Exercises, though one should add that they want their men to be well trained intellectually, not only spiritually. One would imagine that they would sympathize with St. Teresa of Avila when somebody was extolling the virtues of a young woman who wished to join the community. "Yes, yes," said the Saint impatiently, "but has she brains?" The Jesuits, like other orders, take good care not to saddle themselves with persons lacking in intelligence.

A more serious misunderstanding about efficiency should be disposed of. One would imagine that a religious order which lays such stress on obedience would have as many regulations as has the army. This is far from being true. St. Benedict was obliged to write a very detailed Rule because the earlier so-called religious rules were too vague to be of much service. But the Constitutions produced by St. Ignatius might be described as an enunciation of principles rather than a rule, and were in-

[1] This still has unexploited possibilities, as may be seen by any reader of Helen Parry Eden's *A String of Sapphires,* which was published about thirty years ago. But one shudders a little to think what other rhymed catechisms might be.

tended as a directive for superiors rather than as regulations for their subjects. It has often been pointed out that the word "love" occurs much more frequently in the Constitutions than the word obedience. Nevertheless any Jesuit who fails to obey is liable to be dismissed, though this does not mean that he will be. For instance the rather unsatisfactory Francisco Mansilhas, who went to India with Francis Xavier, had his intractable disposition put up with for years, so it is evident that a military obedience was not exacted, this though Xavier was not naturally the most patient of men. The same thing was true of the way that Ignatius himself bore with the difficult Simon Rodriguez, though this leniency may have been, in part, because Rodriguez had been a member of the group since August 15, 1534.

It was, however, never safe to presume too much, as several men discovered to their cost. Obedience was looked for, as is the case in every religious institute. The Jesuits do not seem to have been more exacting than other foundations; the reputation they have obtained for obedience is probably due to the specially explicit vow they take to the Pope.

With regard to obedience, Ignatius expected not only an abnegation of will but also a conformity of judgment. Yet one cannot say that he took a position very different from that of St. Benedict. Neither refused to allow the subject to make representations. Indeed, Ignatius quotes St. Bernard to the effect that a command should be given so tactfully as to suggest that it is not the subject who obeys but his superior. He lays it down that anybody is perfectly free to write to the General — either making an appeal or, more generally, complaining of conditions. The only thing he asks is that the local superior be informed of the grievances that are raised, though he must never be shown the actual letter. That provision is almost more than reasonable, as the local superior should get his first explicit knowledge of the complaint from a letter written him by the General. In this way everybody would be protected against imaginary or frivolous grievances, the superior equally with the subject.

Jesuit poverty did not much differ from that practiced by other orders, except that the Jesuits might be corporately rather well off, while the individual owned nothing, though they seldom, if ever, attained the corporate wealth of some of the abbeys of the Middle Ages. Francis of Assisi had sought to make poverty absolute, but was eventually obliged (or the Franciscans as a group were obliged) to fall back upon the legal subterfuge that placed technical ownership in the hands of a third party, a friend in whom complete trust might be reposed. The Jesuits took a middle ground, more in consonance with realities, though in their case also everything was owned by the community.

As for politics, their Constitutions ordained that Jesuits were "in no way to meddle in public, or secular affairs of princes." During the late sixteenth and the seventeenth centuries, however, politics and religion became so inextricably mingled that often whether a nation was Catholic or Protestant depended upon the ruler who happened to be on the throne. Under such circumstances Jesuits or other Catholics — and the same thing applies to Protestant leaders — were inevitably to some extent entangled in politics, however much they wished to stand aloof. We may see an example of this when the first Jesuit missionaries — Persons and Campion — entered England in 1580. According to their instructions (and to their own desires) they were not to discuss political questions at all, unless it be to express an opinion to some entirely trustworthy friend. But when William Cecil discovered this, he immediately pounced upon it: so a Jesuit could be a politician, so long as he was discreet! Campion, who was taken and executed as a traitor, was, of all men, completely innocent of any sort of political "meddling," and so was Persons at this time. Of him, however, it must be regretfully said that he later threw in his lot with the so-called Spanish party, which favored deposing Queen Elizabeth and putting the daughter of Philip II in her place. That must be admitted to have been treasonable, though it should be added that in later life Persons was of the opinion that it was a blessing for England that the Armada of 1588 had been defeated.

Yet upon the whole the Jesuits were very far from being the political schemers that an inflamed age imagined them to be. After what had happened to Edmund Campion, one of the most beautiful of souls, the missionaries' instructions were framed in such a way as to admit of no political discussion at all. When the last Catholic King of England, James II, put Father Petre upon his council, it was the King himself who was ill advised; Petre always acted with the utmost moderation.

Apart from all this it would be a bit too much to expect that every single member of so large a body of men avoided some dabbling in politics in all places, at all times, and in all circumstances. But the Jesuit politician is almost a complete myth, for it would be impossible to find in the Society anyone who equalled the powerful diplomacy of a Cardinal Cisneros in Spain, of Cardinal Wolsey in England, or the Capuchin "Gray Eminence" who was Cardinal Richelieu's right-hand man and virtually Minister for Foreign Affairs. The unforeseen upshot of the latter's machinations was a set-back to the triumph that Catholicism was on the point of winning, and what seems to be a fatal lesion in the soul of Christendom. Nothing that the Jesuits ever did is even faintly comparable to the politics played by these and some other ecclesiastics.

The Jesuits seem to have got their political reputation mainly from the fact that it became a tradition during the seventeenth and eighteenth centuries that a Jesuit should act as royal confessor. Not unnaturally people imagined that they were pulling political wires, though there seems no case in which these confessors did not carefully restrict themselves to purely spiritual functions, though of course some of them may now and then have been asked for their opinions on other matters, opinions which could not always be refused when a point-blank question was put.

We have seen how Ignatius took care to deal with calumny at once. This is something that has made people consider him unduly sensitive, but it should be remembered that he simply could not afford to let slanders pass. Men in other orders might laugh or shrug things like these off, but Ignatius obtained the Papal bull of 1540 only in the face of a powerful opposition party in the Curia, and Paul III's approbation was, after all, no more than tentative. Therefore Ignatius introduced into the Constitutions a sentence about answering anyone who showed himself a malignant enemy "in written or printed books." Yet Ignatius, unless he possessed prophetic insight, could hardly have guessed how furious the attack was going to be in the eighteenth century. It was Father Retz, the Jesuit General from 1730 to 1750, who amplified what Ignatius had said in the matter by a

special decree. By his time a positive cyclone was blow-
ing, which resulted first in the expulsion of the Jesuits
from the dominions of Portugal, Spain and France, and
eventually in the Papal suppression which was issued to
obtain peace. It seemed final but lasted only until 1814,
after which the Society gradually recovered some of the
ground it had lost and eventually gained so much new
ground that it went on to triumphs that have given it
today a more flourishing condition, by far, than it ever
enjoyed before.

Ignatius often said that he did not want anybody in
the Society whose object was merely that of saving his
own soul. He envisaged an active ministry; for those who
wished to follow the contemplative life there were other
orders — the Carthusians and Trappists, for example —
who engage in no external work though they may accomplish more than anybody suspects by their prayers.
Bishop Hedley, who belonged to the English Black Benedictines, and who therefore is not to be considered a pure
contemplative but whose books belong to our spiritual
classics, put the opposite side of the case when he wrote:
"Perhaps the less a monk thinks about converting the
world and the more he thinks about converting himself,
the more likely will it be that the world will be converted." Yet Hedley's point of view is not really contrary
to that of Ignatius, but merely lays the emphasis somewhat differently. Unless the Jesuit is deeply concerned
about his personal spiritual perfection, his active work
will be largely ineffective.

Before the Constitutions were so much as started, and
Ignatius did not begin to formulate them in writing until
1548, after which he spent three years upon them, a
General for the new religious order had to be elected.
For this purpose all the members of the Company in Italy

assembled in Rome with the exception of Bobadilla who lay ill in Calabria. Faber from Germany and Xavier and Rodriguez from Portugal sent in their votes in writing — an early instance of absentee balloting. Every man, including Ignatius himself, must have well understood that he was the inevitable choice, but despite this, Ignatius continued to hope that he would somehow contrive to escape. Yet when the votes were scrutinized, all but one of them were for Ignatius, and that one of course was his own. He pleaded to be let off, but nobody could think of anybody else who would do. The most that he could accomplish was to persuade the voters to think and pray about the matter for another three days. When the second ballot brought about exactly the same result, Ignatius said he would have to consult his confessor as to what he should do.

This confessor was named Theodore, one of the Observant Franciscans at San Pietro de Montorio. To him Ignatius made so exhaustive a confession that it lasted three days. He tried to prove that he had been a very mediocre kind of a Christian, which may have been true enough of his unregenerate youth, but which was not in the least true of the man he had become. His argument was: how was it possible for him to undertake the government of a group whom he regarded as saints? Father Theodore spared the modesty of Ignatius and did not suggest that he himself was now very holy. Instead he reminded his penitent that St. Peter, despite his denial in the hall of Caiphas, had been chosen by Christ for Pope, the Rock on which the Church was to be built.

In desperation Ignatius seized upon the possibility of another way out: Theodore agreed to defer giving a decision until Ignatius had had an opportunity of making a vigil on the Janiculum at the shrine of Our Lady and, as

St. Peter's name had come up, of praying at the tomb of the Apostle. Yet when, after this, Ignatius went back to his confessor, he was told that to refuse office would be to resist the Holy Ghost.

It shows the stubbornness of Ignatius that he nevertheless did not quite abandon hope. He asked Theodore to pray and think about the question for three days and then send him his final decision in writing. When the letter arrived, however, it was quite definite: there was no further way of refusing the generalship, especially after all the delays; so Ignatius, heavy in heart and still full of a sense of his own unworthiness, was obliged to accept.

Though the Constitutions were not written down until nearly ten years later, an understanding had been reached in 1540 as to what it was they were to contain. The new order abandoned the system of holding chapters, making the government depend entirely upon the General—a monarchical method—and the generalship was to be for life. Less startling as an innovation, but still unique, was that the Jesuit novices (now known as scholastics to distinguish them from lay-brothers), after completing their long novitiate of two years, and after that finishing their courses in philosophy, give three years to teaching, before proceeding to the study of theology.[1]

---

[1] This was not a settled part of the original plan. We find that even the first experimental draft of the *Ratio Studiorum*, which appeared in 1586 recommended that the scholastics should teach Humanities even *before* they commenced their philosophical studies, and that the 1599 edition, while allowing this in exceptional cases, made the teaching of Humanities come *after* the completion of philosophy. This is normal today, but the three-year term of teaching may, but only for very good reasons, be shortened, as it may also be lengthened. In a few instances it can be drawn out to as many as five years. About such matters the Constitutions are elastic.

It goes without saying that this period of teaching lengthens that of the scholastic's preparation, and it might be thought to be, in some respects, inadvisable. While teaching, the scholastic runs the risk of forgetting a good deal of what he had learned, and as theology calls for a philosophical foundation, the interruption might seem a mistake. In practice, however, the system seems to work well. The scholastic teacher lives among ordained priests and in many instances probably learns more theology from their conversation than he would have mastered in a classroom. When eventually he does enter a classroom for the formal study of theology, it is with a mind that has matured. Indeed, his whole outlook may be considerably enriched by his own practical work as a teacher.

Other innovations were that the Jesuits wore no religious habit, merely the garb of secular priests; moreover, they were debarred from accepting ecclesiastical dignities, though now and then, when there is exceptionally good reason, one of them may be raised to the episcopacy. However, there is really nothing very new about this, for other orders, too, are reluctant to give up their own men for the performance of work that may be performed as well by priests taken from the diocesan clergy. A cardinalate also is now and then accepted by a Jesuit, but this of course is rarely offered.

The greatest innovations introduced by Ignatius — greater even than the abandonment of a religious habit — were the surrender of the capitular system and, most of all, of the choral saying of the Office. Yet this was necessary if the Jesuits were to do their distinctive work, as this required their moving freely to any point of the world, in groups or pairs or even singly, though it need hardly be said that the duty of privately saying the Di-

vine Office remained.[1] Paul IV (who was elected Pope
in 1555, holding office until his death in 1559) strongly
disapproved of the Jesuits' giving up the choir, and commanded that in this respect they do as other religious
did. Obedience was given to the stormy octogenarian,
but as his order was only by word of mouth, the Jesuits
discarded the choir as soon as he died.

As we have seen, Ignatius accepted the generalate of
the Company with the greatest reluctance. In 1551 he
pleaded that he be allowed to resign on account of his
infirmities, though he was only sixty and perhaps, if he
was born in 1493, not even as old as that. Long before
1551 the restriction of the new order to sixty members
had been removed, so that there was rapid growth and
an increase in the general's administrative duties. As he
was so very slow a writer, in the sense of writing any important letter several times, and as his responsibilities
made necessary the writing of thousands of letters and
instructions, he would have been utterly unable to cope
with his burdens had he not obtained the young and
highly efficient Juan de Polanco as his secretary. When
he begged to resign the Jesuit Fathers insisted that Ignatius remain at his post but assigned Peter Ribadeneira
and Jerome Nadal to act as his assistants. Although Ignatius was quite willing that these men act on their own
authority, they revered Ignatius so much that each laid
aside any plans of his own if these did not accord with
the wishes of the General. On his part Ignatius was always inviting others to set him right and to correct his
faults. To the fiery Bobadilla he was to write: "I well

---

[1] Paul III dispensed Ignatius from even this on account of his poor
health. But the dispensation extended only to him personally.

recall that on the day of your profession, I earnestly begged all the Company, that in everything where they saw me fail, they would . . . have the goodness to remind me of my failures so that I might be able to reform myself in the Lord." From this it is clear that he was the reverse of a martinet; but his moral ascendency was never questioned by anybody.

In the succeeding chapters an attempt will be made to indicate how the work of the Company broadened out, and that from the very start, though the account given in so small a book as this cannot be other than episodic. Yet as this will carry us into some general historical observations, and a consideration of work done in various parts of the world, it will be enough to say here that everything was controlled by Ignatius from his little room in Rome. His interest in all that was going on was once put by him as a wish to know how many fleas were biting his sons in other places. Yet that he was not exclusively concerned with his order is shown by the fact that he established a house for fallen women and another for unprotected girls and was, despite his imperfect knowledge of Italian, an effective preacher at the times when he ascended the pulpit. In addition he raised funds for orphanages and devoted himself to the care and protection of Jewish converts.

In 1550 he had succeeded in establishing in Rome, with the help of an initial gift supplied him by Francis Borgia, Duke of Gandia, a seminary for the education of an elite clergy called the Roman College, later to be rechristened as the Gregorian University. Two years later he opened the Germanicum, a college for the training of German priests in learning and piety, since there was at that time no place in the Empire where they might be formed. For both of these institutions Ignatius was constantly in search of funds, and he extended to the students the same care that he showed toward the members of his own order, overseeing even their physical welfare and the regulation of their fasts.

As there will be no further occasion for returning to Ignatius himself, a word must be said about his death. For a long time he had suffered, off and on, from an ailment of the stomach which none of the doctors he consulted was able to diagnose. Often the pain made him very weak, despite which he kept steadily at work. Because of this no great alarm was felt, for his was a chronic condition and when it became acute, in a day or two he was able to go on as before. All this should be remembered when we come to his death.

A critical condition was reached at the end of July, 1556, but the two doctors who examined him could see no special cause for worry, believing that he would survive this crisis, as he had survived others, though Ignatius himself was sure he was about to die. On July 28th he received Holy Communion and in the afternoon he asked his secretary, Father Polanco, to go to Pope Paul IV to obtain the Papal blessing. But Polanco,[1] having been reassured by the doctors, and wishing to get off some important letters to Spain, asked if his going to the Pope could not be put off until the following day. "The sooner you go, the better I shall be satisfied," said Ignatius; "however, do as you wish." And Polanco took him at his word. It is curious how meekly Ignatius, even in this very important matter, submitted to his secre-

---

[1] The admirable man seems to have come to think of himself as indispensable — which was very nearly true. It is a wonder that not he but Laynez was elected to succeed Ignatius.

tary, laying aside his own better judgment. Rarely has humility been shown so clearly.

The infirmarian passed the next few nights in Loyola's room, but he had been doing so for some time, and he noticed nothing out of the way. But on July 31st at daybreak it was apparent that Ignatius was in his agony, whereupon Polanco hurried to the Vatican for the Pope's blessing. The end came more quickly than was expected, and by the time that Polanco returned Ignatius Loyola was dead, having passed away without Paul IV's blessing or Extreme Unction or Viaticum.

A post-mortem examination revealed that the Saint's intestines and liver were in such a condition that the doctors were astonished that he had been able to live so long at all. Yet even on his deathbed Ignatius had continued to work, to the extent of giving some business directions. We may be sure that there were a few things about his death that Ignatius would have wished to be otherwise, and we can regret them too; but we cannot but admire a man who died so serenely, and in harness. He would of course have wished to die with all the consolations of religion; as it was he died in almost complete dereliction, except for whatever God may have given without human intervention. It was a strange way along which the dapper young Spanish soldier had been led to sanctity.

Nine

The Missionary Effort

THIS EFFORT BEGAN even before the Company of
Jesus was approved by Paul III's bull, the *Regimini militantis Ecclesiae,* on September 27, 1540, and of course an
even longer time before the new order had elected any
General. Yet for some time John III, the King of Portugal,
had been asking Ignatius to send six of the members of
the as yet unconstituted Company as missionaries to Goa
in India. To this Ignatius could simply throw up his hands
and say that the group he had at his disposal — and they
were still not canonically at his disposal at all — was so
small that six men were out of the question. He did,
however, with great generosity and courage, promise
Pedro de Mascarenhas, King John's ambassador in Rome,
to let him have two. Of those selected Bobadilla was
one.

Bobadilla, however, never went, as he suddenly came
down with sciatica; so Ignatius, who was himself ill at
the time, turned to Francis Xavier, asking him to take
Bobadilla's place and go with Simon Rodriguez in the
entourage of Mascarenhas to Lisbon. The instant reply
was, "Here I am — ready," to which Ignatius answered,
"Go, and set all on fire." What seemed a mere accident
started the greatest of missionaries on his astounding career. The date should be borne in mind: it was March 14,

1540, five months before there was any formally recognized Company of Jesus.

We have seen how Ignatius signalized his conversion in 1521, by going, after his stay at Montserrat, on a pilgrimage to the Holy Land, something that was more than an ordinary pilgrimage, as he attempted to convert the Moslems there. That had inevitably failed, but the idea of it remained with him, for in 1537 he induced those who joined him at the University of Paris to go out with him for a second, more carefully planned, campaign, to which they bound themselves by a vow. It was only the outbreak of war between Venice and the Turks that prevented this — and providentially so — as the efforts of the Jesuits were perforce made in Europe, where they were most wanted.

Nevertheless, the missionary dream had by no means faded, which was the reason the Jesuits were so prompt in responding to the request of King John III of Portugal for men to work for the evangelization of the places in the Orient where he had established his colonies. That is why the story of the Jesuit missionary effort opens in March, 1540, despite the fact the Papal approbation of their new order, though it could be confidently counted upon, was not officially conferred until the bull Paul III issued five months later.

Perhaps I may be pardoned for running ahead of my story to say a brief word about a missionary effort of still greater importance that was to come only a few years later. This was the work done by St. Peter Canisius — who had been trained first by Faber, then by Ignatius — in repelling the surging Protestant wave that threatened to engulf Germany and Poland. Had it not been for Canisius and his associates not only the whole

of Northern Europe would have been taken by the Reform, but the hands of the Huguenots in France would
have been so immensely strengthened that, so far as we
are able to see, France would also have become a
Protestant country, leaving only Italy and Spain and
Portugal under Catholic obedience.

I much regret that this can only be touched on here.
But perhaps I can afford to dismiss it briefly because,
though most Catholics — at least in English-speaking
countries — are not very well informed as to just what
happened, they are at least aware that a large part of
Germany was saved for the Catholic Church, along with
most of Hungary, nearly all Austria, at least a half of the
Low Countries (even to this day Holland is one-third
Catholic), and the whole of a then most precariously
held Poland.

This was of course not the achievement of one man,
even a man so great as Canisius, but for the sake of con-
serving space we may confine ourselves to him, as the
leader of the undertaking. He traveled on horseback from
the Rhine in the West to the Vistula in the East, inces-
santly at work to achieve one sole object, the preservation (and restoration) of the Faith in those vast territories. Father Broderick in his *Progress of the Jesuits*
(which covers the years 1556–1579) describes him as
"the Great Drudge of the Counter-Reformation." He was
joined by many Spanish Fathers, in response to his appeal for workers, so that sixty years later, there were
well over 2,000 Jesuits engaged in the Empire, and they
had established 120 colleges, seminaries and missions
within it. The Reformation, though not conquered, had
been held at bay and much lost ground was regained.

Father Broderick says that Canisius was the first Jesuit to write a book (he does not count the *Spiritual Exercises* as a book), about which more in just a moment. I pause first to make a jest that I trust will be accepted as such and not be resented; but it sometimes seems, because of the enormous Jesuit literary output that many members of the order have brought themselves to believe that they must publish something if they are to get to heaven. The contribution of Canisius was a catechism (or rather three catechisms, each for youths of a different age), and this proved to be the most effective method of counteracting the little manual by means of which Luther, who was after all a man of genius, had popularized his heresy. But in addition Canisius constantly preached, founded a number of colleges, and by unremitting toil, succeeded in stemming the Protestant Reformation. His life was one of the hardest possible work, and contains relatively few dramatic incidents for the biographer; but not in the slightest way does he deserve anything but our thankful reverence.

There is drama aplenty when we look at the work done by the Jesuit missionaries in Elizabethan England. But it is no belittling of the Jesuits to say that they came after the priests whom William Allen had trained in his seminary in the Low Countries. These seminarians were never permitted to forget the fate that almost certainly awaited them, for paintings of prisoners stretched on the rack, and even scenes of the butchery of Tyburn representing these in unflinchingly realistic detail, hung in their seminary classroom and the refectory. The Jesuits who went to England were not brought up with the sight of such horrors before their eyes, though they knew about them, for in their novitiate they had no idea to what work they would be assigned after ordination. It was in

1580 that Campion and Persons with ten seminary priests
and a lay brother left Rome for England where their
activities in eluding the priest-hunters and making contact with the hidden Catholics of the country have furnished the material for hundreds of books. Campion was
hanged, drawn and quartered in December 1581, and
many of those who followed him also suffered torture
and death.

Nor did this quite end after the Stuarts came to the
throne, though executions were then fewer. In the Gunpowder Plot during the reign of James I, it emerged that
one of the conspirators, having had some qualms of conscience, had asked the advice of his Jesuit confessor
(without actually confessing the matter as a sin), and
had given his confessor permission to consult his superior. Since both priests judged that to disclose what
they had learned would be to break the secret of the
confessional, they were charged with high treason, on
the ground that they were accessories before the fact. In
this instance it might be admitted that there was some
kind of basis for the Crown's prosecution. But there
was none whatever in the case of the so-called Catholic Plot for the assassination of Charles II which Titus
Oates pretended to have uncovered. Yet about thirty
people, eight of them priests and several of them Jesuits, were hanged before the lying imposter Oates was
unmasked. The King himself, though he was aware that
the plot was entirely fictitious, dared not stand out against
the frenzy of the populace; yet he was himself drawn
toward Catholicism, and was received into the Church
on his deathbed. The feeling against Catholics was such
that it was believed that they had started the Great Fire
of London that occurred about this time. The inscription

charging this has long since been removed from the
monument, but a hundred years after the Great Fire it
was still there, leading Alexander Pope to write:

Where London's column, pointing at the skies
Like a tall bully, lifts its head and lies.

Yet this was a period that supposedly marks the nadir
of Catholic fortunes in England, and incidentally of that
of the Jesuits, who were said to have a hand in every
plot. Charles II's brother, James II, had been openly a
Catholic long before his accession, but though he managed to suppress the insurrection of his bastard nephew,
the Duke of Monmouth, James' discretion was much less
than his courage, with the consequence that he was de-
posed by a subsequent intrigue and the throne of England made, as it has been since 1688, a Protestant perqui-
site. After that, the Catholics in England, until the extraordinary revival of modern times, were a cowed and
steadily diminishing minority, among whom their few
priests could, at best, hope only to maintain the little
ground they had. The country gave no opportunities for
missionary work on the part of Jesuits or any other group.
Yet what had been done so heroically during the late
sixteenth century was far from being a failure; rather
it must be considered as laying the foundation for triumphs still concealed and for still greater triumphs
which, by God's grace, may lie in the future.

But I leave all this to deal with the astonishing effort
of Francis Xavier in the Orient. As we have seen, John III
of Portugal, acting under the advice of Gouvea, the rector
of Sainte-Barbe's College (and, it may be suspected, of
his queen, if indeed she was the lady with whom Ignatius had been airily and romantically in love when he

was in his twenties), asked Ignatius to supply missionaries for Goa in India, with the result that Rodriguez and Xavier were despatched to Lisbon in the train of the Portuguese ambassador.

Once the two men arrived, the King and Catalina, his wife, were so taken with them that they wanted to keep them in Portugal. Goa already had some Franciscan missionaries and others could be sent to India. In the end a compromise was reached: Rodriguez stayed in Portugal and Xavier sailed for India in the company of Paul of Camerino, a Jesuit priest, Diego Rodriguez, a lay-brother, and a somewhat oafish young scholastic named Francisco Mansilhas, whom it might be flattering too much to call Francis' Sancho Panza. Far from being of much use, Mansilhas was to prove almost a millstone round the neck of the fiery Xavier.

When Francis Xavier sailed for India in April, 1541, he was thirty-five; eleven years later he was dead on a lonely little island off the coast of China. In between he had done a work that marks him as the greatest of missionaries since St. Paul, one which has inspired thousands of other men and women. Over and over again we come across those whose apostolic zeal had been kindled by him, as is true even of the pioneer priests of the United States. His letters — some of which were published without his authorization even while he was alive — show him a flame of fire that nothing could quench. In one of them he bursts out with: "How I should like to go through the universities of Europe shouting like a madman about the souls that are being lost. How many there are in such places who are thinking only of getting a high position in the Church through their reputation for learning, instead of using their acquirements for the common good.

If only they would leave their miserable ambitions and say, 'Lord, here am I. Send me where Thou wilt — even to India!' how much better their own state would be when they come to die." By the narrowest squeeze he had escaped the comfortable life of a canon of Pamplona; how incomparably greater was the ambition that now consumed him.

What he accomplished is all the more remarkable when we discover with what obstacles he had to contend. The toughest of all was the attitude of many of the Portuguese officials in India. These he found to be rotten with venality, men who cared for nothing except amassing a fortune by exploiting the natives with whom they came into contact. They may not have been so successful in their rapacity as was the Englishman Robert Clive of the eighteenth century, who was able to retire when he was thirty-five with a fortune of over £300,000, or of his near contemporary Warren Hastings, who did even better for himself, but was tried for his misdemeanors in Westminster Hall, where Burke delivered against him one of the most celebrated of his speeches; even so the Portuguese were rather good at feathering their own nests. Moreover their luxurious mode of life with a harem of concubines gave such scandal that an almost impassable barrier was set against the conversion of the Hindus.

Time after time Francis complained about men of this type to the King himself, with the result perhaps that an administrator of a higher grade was sent out. But it took about a year for a letter between Lisbon and Goa to arrive, and the Portuguese operated over an immense territory. In many of their posts they lived openly as Jews or Mohammedans and were virtually immune from official correction. In the end Xavier despairingly suggested the establishment of the Inquisition, but that was an institution incapable of dealing with more than a very few of the cases that created trouble in the Portuguese dominions, and it never functioned except sporadically. The minor officials, the moment they were fairly safe from surveillance, went on exactly as before. There were honest men among them, some of an inflexible honesty, but the prevailing tone was that of corruption. Francis may have been inclined to magnify any departure from an absolute probity, but it is historically ascertainable that the personal character of many officials was anything but elevated. Only a man like Xavier would have not lost heart among such people.

In India Francis missed a great opportunity, however, which he was temperamentally unfitted to utilize: he would have nothing to do with the Brahmins, regarding them as imposters, out for their own gain and the maintenance of their ascendancy. To approach them successfully called for a patience that Francis lacked, not to mention a sympathetic understanding of their intricate customs and an insight into the philosophy that underlay them. As we shall see, the Jesuits of the seventeenth century showed themselves astonishingly adept in a mastery of methods which Francis would never bother to learn. The high-born Basque gentleman and the master of arts of the University of Paris confined himself to working among the poorest and most ignorant of the natives.

He had what seemed to be more than ample justification: thousands of the pearl fishers on the southeast tip of India had already accepted baptism, but merely as a means of securing the dubious protection of the Portu-

guese against warlike Indian marauders. These so-called
Christians knew nothing, or virtually nothing, about the
Faith they found it politically convenient to profess.
They continued in their old ways, and what religious
ideas they had were far removed from the lofty philosophy attained by many Brahmins, and were of the grossest
superstition.

Still it must be remembered that the Brahmins themselves regarded *suttee* — the practice (though not the
obligation) that many newly made widows had of throwing themselves upon the funeral pyres of their husbands
— with full approval. This was not because women were
looked upon as a degraded sex, but because wifely devotion was thought their highest virtue. The Hindu, at
his best, is the most religious of men, and his religion has
been expounded in detail (and with an accuracy to which
I can testify by my own knowledge of what India was
sixty years ago) by the eighteenth-century Abbé Dubois.
The British, during their rule, suppressed many things
like *suttee*, and the new Indian government has gone
further than the British ever ventured to go in changing
the Indian way of life. But at his worst, though the Hindu
is still gentle and kind, he is inclined to a soft sort of
corruption.

Sex was in the very air Xavier breathed, and one did
not have to go more than a mile on the public roads to
encounter phallic emblems, placed where even children
could see them. Moreover, the great Hindu temples —
all on the plan of an immense flattened pyramid, and all
surrounded by a colonnade with a great pool at the
center — were carved all over with bas-reliefs of the most
explicit eroticism. So also is it with what Europeans describe as "temple prostitution" but to which Hinduism

gives a very different name, calling the girls engaged in it *devadasis,* which means "servants of God." I realize what is behind all this, and that for them it has the spiritual meaning that the body is the handmaid of the soul. But Francis Xavier naturally regarded all this with nothing but horror.

This was so also with something of a very different kind, one which was indeed shocking but which modern India has prohibited.[1] This was the marriage of young girls, sometimes while they were infants, to grown men. In a case of that sort the tiny "wife" continued to live with her parents until nubile. The idea here was that, if marriage was consummated at the first signs of puberty, virginity would be guaranteed. But if, even while a wife was still in her infancy, her husband happened to die, she was condemned to a life-long widowhood, which usually meant a life-long drudgery. Only during the last couple of generations have men of "advanced" notions been found willing to marry virgin widows.

Mixed up with all this, in the case of the illiterate, was a good deal of devil-worship and magic. Every field in Southern India contains a stake on the top of which dangles a *chatti,* or large earthernware pot, dotted with white spots. These are imagined to be a protection against the evil eye, and in particular against the numerous godlets in their open-air shrines. These idols are surrounded by life-sized clay horses, on one of which they ride at evening; and woe to any belated peasant they catch! The site of Mount Sion, the house my Protestant missionary father built in the Madras Presidency, on a slight elevation in the plain, had been such a shrine.

[1] The British *raj* followed a policy of tolerating as much as possible. The new Indian regime has made it unlawful for a youth to marry before he is 18, and for a girl 16. This is better than the law in most of our States.

Most of the people were not only illiterate but incredibly poor. Dressed in nothing but a loin-cloth the *ryot*, or peasant, still toils to wring a living from the soil of South India, using only the most primitive sort of a plough and depending upon irrigation, drawing the water (also in a very primitive style) from a tank filled at the monsoon season or from a river. The native women of the lower classes were a bit better clothed than their menfolk, but reserved their graceful *saris* and bodices for special "dress-up" occasions. None was so poor, however, that she did not have gaudy earrings of gold, but, except among the well-to-do, only of a shell of that precious metal. These constituted her dowry, to receive which her ears were pierced in infancy so that the lobes could be gradually enlarged with leaden weights. Of these not very valuable earrings she was immensely proud. But even her best *saris* were of cheap material, whereas those of well-to-do wives had silver, and even gold, woven into them. No Indian wife ever had to wail that she had nothing to wear. Her *sari* never went out of fashion, and when at last it became threadbare, she simply burned it and with the residium of metal left could buy another.

The fuel of the poor was usually only dried cow dung, and cow dung mixed with water was used (as no doubt it still is), to keep the beaten mud-floors of their houses cool and (strange though this may sound) clean. I know, because in our mission-station we used it. On these bare floors most of the people sleep, using nothing but a mat of plaited palm leaves, but sometimes being able to use a bed which had no mattress, only a crisscross of rope.

Francis Xavier did not permit himself any relaxations, but was always at work, traveling from the west to the east of Southern India by a swift-sailing catamaran, though at least once he crossed from the pearl-fisheries to Travancore by foot, when he must have gone over the part that was my boyhood's home. Sometimes, too, he may have used one of the springless bullock-drawn *vandis,* whose pace is a couple of miles an hour, though he says nothing about this and may have considered a *vandi* too luxurious for him. This vehicle I was well acquainted with, and I can testify that it is anything but a comfortable means of transportation.

Along a strip of southeastern India, between the mountain range called the Ghats and the sea, there was an ancient Christian community which claimed to have been founded by St. Thomas the Apostle. Thomas may indeed have visited India, as tradition says — and what purports to be his tomb is shown near Madras — but, if so, his converts were subsequently subverted by Nestorianism. Madras, by the way, great city though it now is, is of fairly recent origin, and its name is supposed to be a corruption of *Madre de Dios,* a fact of special interest to me as Madras happens to be my birthplace. But as for the Nestorian Christians of Travancore (sometimes called the Syrian), Francis Xavier must have run into them now and then without making any attempt to bring them back to Catholic orthodoxy, his mission being for the heathen. Only now are large segments of the Nestorians submitting to the Roman obedience. Francis probably decided (and quite rightly) that to accomplish anything in Travancore so much time would be needed that he would have to give up everything else. As he had gone to the East for the sake of the heathen, he would not permit himself to be distracted from that work.

In his many letters to Ignatius, Francis was no Abbé Dubois, for hardly ever does he give any account of Indian customs, except in the rare instances when he had to explain them in order to indicate their bearing upon what he was doing. If he often makes indignant complaints about the Portuguese officials, for the natives themselves he had no blame but only love. He could not but see, however, that many of the Tamils were rather poor specimens of humanity. It was hard to get into their heads any very clear concept of Christian truth, and he recognized that not much more could be done than to give them a little elementary instruction, teach them the Creed and the Ten Commandments and then baptize them. But he baptized them by the thousands, often spending a whole day doing nothing else, and stopping only because his arms ached.[1] Nevertheless, his work and that of the Jesuits who went out to join him endured, so that today there are thousands of Tamils who regard him as their spiritual father. Even the heathen had so great an admiration for him that, after his death, in some places he obtained the cult accorded one of their minor gods. But as I believe that there are probably about 3,000 members of the Hindu pantheon — many of whom are now completely forgotten, even locally — perhaps the honor was not so great as it might seem.

Eventually Francis Xavier became so disgusted with the Portuguese officials in India that he decided to push further to the east; this was at all events one of the factors that operated with him. Yet he considered Goa his headquarters, and it was to Goa that he always returned after his missionary journeys. He was also fired with the idea of winning the whole Orient for Christ. One is staggered by the audacity of so grandiose a concept.

---

[1] Many years later the right arm that he used was severed from his body at Goa and sent to Rome, from where it was sent throughout the United States only a very few years ago.

His first excursions were made to some of the islands of the South Pacific — or perhaps they are reckoned as belonging to the Malay Archipelago — to Celebes and Ceram and the Islands of the Moors, but for some strange reason he did not go to the nearer Sumatra or Java. Borneo he may have thought too big to tackle; and as for the Philippines, they were claimed by Spain and so left unvisited by him. There were many other islands that he might have gone to, had it not been that it was always part of his plan to settle a Jesuit wherever he went to follow up his work, and he simply did not have enough men. Moreover, the date of departure and arrival of the slow sailing ships of the time had to depend upon the intervals between monsoons. He made Malacca his base, though one secondary to Goa.

At Malacca he got acquainted with a young Japanese named Anjiro, whom he converted and took back for training to the college he had established in Goa, and whom some think he may even have received into the Society. (This, however, is unlikely as Anjiro, now Paul of the Holy Faith, seems to have had a wife in Japan.) But Francis certainly counted upon using Paul as an interpreter, for, despite stories still current about Xavier's possessing the gift of tongues, it is evident from what he says in his letters that this is without foundation. He never learned to speak except brokenly even the Tamil of Southern India.

From what Francis learned from Paul of the Holy Faith about Japan — much of it misleading or not quite understood — he decided that he would change his tactics when he reached that country. It was actually governed by nobles, or the greater Buddhist abbots, many of whom, like the nobles, had armed retainers. Each of these nota-

bles was largely autonomous in his own territory; but
what Francis gathered from Paul was that the country
was governed by a "king," whom he naturally thought
of as like European monarchs. He did not grasp the
strange Japanese political system, or realize that the
Mikado or Emperor counted for next to nothing and that
the governing power was in the hands of the Shogun,
or head of the army. The situation was not unlike that
of the Merovingian Franks before Charlemagne, when
the mayor of the palace, rather than the nominal king,
was the personage who counted. Had Francis Xavier
comprehended this, it would have been the Shogun and
not the Emperor whom he would have sought out. As it
was, after establishing friendly relations with some of the
diamyos or nobles, and a few Buddhist abbots, he set out
for Kyoto, then the capital of Japan.

When he arrived at the royal palace he was rudely dis-
illusioned. The Mikado, now a mere figurehead, was not
to be seen, because the palace attendants would not admit Francis until he had given them presents, and with
these he had come unprovided. But it did not really matter: the figurehead of a Mikado was reduced to supple-
menting his very meager income by writing out sacred
texts or musical scores, certified to be by him, or selling
bottles of his bath water. All that Xavier and his companions saw was a glimpse or two of the royal concubines
in their threadbare kimonas. He left Kyoto having accomplished nothing.

Even Paul of the Holy Faith eventually defected, for
this promising young man went to the bad a few years
after Francis left Japan; turning river pirate, he was killed
on one of his raids in China. But though the converts
Francis made in Japan were not many when compared

with the thousands so easily won in India, most of them were of exceptionally high grade. Xavier could never say enough in his letters in praise of them, his favorite term for them being "my darlings." As a nation they stood out for their politeness, but after conversion, they showed the most exquisite courtesy. His judgment — and how right he was! — was that they would be hard to convert, but that once they were Christians they would prove unshakable.

The converts he did make acquired a sound knowledge of their religion and were zealous in their practice. What good Catholics they were appeared when there burst upon them in the seventeenth century what was perhaps the most savage persecution that any people has ever had to endure. This was instigated by the Calvinist Dutch traders and sprang from the commercial rivalry between them and the Portuguese. As a consequence, unspeakable cruelties — cruelties sometimes unmentionable because of their obscenity — were often used to extirpate Catholicism. Hundreds of men and women suffered martyrdom, and there were very few apostates, though among these was the Jesuit provincial himself. However, he repented and, upon returning to the Faith, suffered the hideous martyrdom of what was called the "Pit."

How great was the ruin may be gauged from the fact that by that time there were about 150 Jesuits laboring in Japan, and with them four times as many catechists. There were 300 churches, two colleges for the sons of the nobility, a house of studies for Jesuits and a novitiate. All were swept away at a blow, or so it seemed. But the Japanese Christians, devoid of priests, went "underground," retaining only the sacrament of baptism, mak-

ing their confessions to one another, although of course
not receiving sacramental absolution, and doing their
best to impart something of a religious color to the merely
"natural" marriages now possible. This state of affairs
lasted until about 1865; then it was discovered, the moment Japan was thrown open again, that at least 50,000
people had been faithful to Christianity in secret. One
can only gaze in awe at such iron fortitude.[1] After that it
is not hard to understand why to Francis Xavier the
Japanese were his darlings.

He did not remain very long in the country, but this
was because there had occurred to him a new way of
winning Japan. He decided that, as it was from China
that Japanese culture and religion had been derived, he
should first arm himself with Chinese prestige. In his
mind there were a number of fallacies, mixed with some
truths. As Japan had become his dearest love, he thought
to turn its flank by first converting China. He brought
himself to believe that, should he win over the Emperor
of China — and why not? — Japan would drop like a ripe
peach into his lap. After all, he was still only in his middle forties, and his energy had no limits. One may feel
aghast at his intrepidity, but his idea was not so chimerical as it may appear. Nor was Japan all; his object was
to win the whole of the Orient for Christ, and this was
something that he might have gone a long way toward
accomplishing had he had twenty more years of life
(thirty were quite possible) — a long life and mountains
of good luck. He had made tens of thousands of converts in India and the islands of the South Pacific; nobody

---

[1] It may not be amiss to note here that the first and major victims of
the atom bomb at Nagasaki and Hiroshima were Japanese Catholics.

need smile if he were now thinking in terms of millions. If there had been anybody capable of effecting such a scheme, Francis Xavier was the man.

It need not be said that he could have had no conception of the immensity of China, but at least he was well aware that he would need an army of helpers to evangelize China, or, for that matter, even Japan. These he was confident would offer themselves as soon as the possibilities were made known in Europe. So first he would return to Goa, partly to see how matters were progressing there, but mainly to obtain credentials as an ambassador to the Chinese Emperor. Without such credentials he was aware that he would not even be admitted into China, a country absolutely closed to all Europeans, but as the representative of the king of Portugal he would have to be received at Peking. He was sure that armed with such documents, and by the grace of God, he would, if not convert the Emperor, at least obtain permission to preach the Faith. He was no doubt much too sanguine, but far from being a fool he was one of the most intelligent men who ever lived, and besides extraordinary personal charm had the beautiful manners of the aristocrat.

As it would have taken too long — at least two years and more probably three — to wait for credentials signed by King John III of Portugal, he accepted instead papers from the king's representative in the Orient, the governor of Goa. That Francis did so was natural, yet it would have been better had he written to the king and awaited the necessary documents from Portugal. His mistake came out when the commandant at Malacca was not satisfied with the papers in Francis' possession, and refused to return them (as a recently appointed man he was inclined to be officious). It was in vain that Francis Xavier informed him that he was not merely the Portuguese ambassador but had arrived at Goa commissioned as nuncio by the Pope. He had been given this dignity some years before in case he had the chance to go to Ethiopia; as in India and Japan he had had no occasion to make use of his nunciature, he had never so much as mentioned it, not even to the Franciscan bishop of Goa. Now the commandant of Malacca refused to believe that the dignity had ever been conferred upon him.

That he was interfering with a papal nuncio involved *ipso facto* excommunication, but the commandant believed that all this was bluff, and Francis Xavier had not brought the papal document with him. The man's decision was that Xavier might proceed to China, but it would have to be in the character of an ordinary priest and at his own risk. This, he thought, would effectually put an end to the project, for both men were well aware that there was no getting into the country unless it was as the emissary of King John.

Little did the commandant understand Francis Xavier. The missionary determined to make the attempt, even under such a handicap. He was resourceful and he counted upon God's providing a way, if that was His will. Though China itself lay impenetrably closed, there was a little island named Sancian, within sight of Canton, where Portuguese traders were permitted to put in at certain seasons of the year, so that Chinese junks might go out to them. This "bootleg" trade was officially winked at, on the condition that the ships sailed away at the approach of winter, leaving on the island not so much as a vestige of the shacks that had sheltered their crews; there was no question of any of them putting into Canton itself.

This being the case, Francis tried to get one of the
junks to ferry him to the mainland. Here he was taking a
considerable chance, for the captain of the junk might,
after accepting his fee, get his sailors to cut Xavier's
throat, rather than land him at Canton, where he might
have his own head cut off. However, the captain may
have thought it prudent not to get into a scuffle with the
athletic Francis, and so failed to put in an appearance.

By the time the Portuguese ships sailed away that year,
Francis had fallen ill. He could have been taken off
Sancian by one of the departing ships, but as he refused
to go, there was nothing for it but to leave him to his
fate. No doubt by this time the supplies of the trading
fleet were running low; even so, one would have supposed
that a little could have been spared for a very sick man.
All that Francis got was that, at the last moment, somebody handed him — of all things in the world — a handful of almonds! What Francis thought he could do now
is impossible to imagine; but by this time he may have
been delirious, incapable of thought but as stubborn as
ever.

The date of his death is given in the breviary as December 3, 1552, which is the date on which the Church
celebrates the feast day of the Saint, though, oddly
enough, it is said there, in the second nocturn, that he
died on the 2nd. The only people left to look after him
were a Chinese boy and a young Tamil named Antonio. They heard him muttering in several languages,
but as Antonio knew Latin, one may surmise that mostly
Francis used the Basque that would have been utterly
unintelligible to the Tamil. His last words were the line
from the *Te Deum: In te, Domine, speravi: non confundar*

in aeternum. By that time his mind had cleared, even if before then it had wandered for a while.

The two young Orientals buried Francis Xavier at once, pouring quicklime over his body, as they knew that when the Portuguese returned a year later, they would want to carry away his bones. But when he was dug up, a perfectly fresh corpse was found. This was reburied at Malacca, where it remained another year, in a climate which normally is torrid and humid. When the body was disinterred again, to be entombed in the Jesuit church at Goa, it was still quite incorrupt. This is still its condition, though it now looks rather mummified. Incorruptibility is not demanded for canonization, though it has frequently occurred among dead saints, but Francis Xavier's is a case without parallel; one is staggered that the quicklime had no effect. There is also cause for wonder that three burials, all in the heat of the Orient, and the passage of four hundred years have done no more than to make his body a bit shriveled, with flesh of a texture something like that of wood.

Ten

Change of Tactics

THE CRUCIAL PROBLEM of missionary work in India, and one that exists to this day, is that of inducing the upper classes to become Christians. This is largely because they are *not* upper classes as the term is usually understood; they are castes, having not merely social position — still less being always wealthy — but invested with a religious character. For instance, even in sixteenth-century Spain, where aristocracy was more rigid than elsewhere, it was not quite impossible for a man to obtain a title either through signal service or royal favor, rare though such elevation might be. Similarly in the England of that time, another highly aristocratic country, we find Thomas Cromwell, the son of a drunken inn-keeper, rising to a barony and finally an earldom, regarded all the while as a parvenu by his fellow nobles but with power second only to the king's. Earlier in the same reign, a man whose only claim was that his father had been the first Tudor's standard-bearer at the battle of Bosworth, became successively a knight, a viscount and eventually Duke of Suffolk, in which status he ventured to marry Henry VIII's sister, queen-dowager of France. And William Cecil, Queen Elizabeth I's famous minister, became Lord Burghley, though it is by no means certain who was his grandfather.

124

Now in India there are no titles except those that were conferred by the British government and those of the rajahs, who are sometimes not of the very highest caste. The highest caste of all are of course the Brahmins, priests, philosophers and guardians of the *arcana* of Hinduism. They are not usually very rich, for those who make fortunes are commonly beneath them in standing, though to the lowest castes (and especially the "untouchables") all avenues for material advancement are completely closed. But the caste of the Brahmins inclines to make them extremely arrogant; in any event they are, except in exceptionally rare instances, impermeable to any religious notions other than their own.

Francis Xavier ran across Brahmins from time to time and in one of his letters gives an account of a meeting he had with a group of them in the vast temple of Madura. He set them down as imposters and made absolutely no attempt to win them, not even striking up the kind of friendship he established in Japan with a few of the Buddhist abbots. In short, he wiped them off his slate; so far as he was concerned they did not exist.

All this is understandable but was rather erroneous, for if Xavier had had the patience to discover the facts, he would have learned that India is, in many ways, the most religious country in the world; indeed the Brahmins themselves, whatever their faults may have been, were capable of being reached, for there were points of contact between their beliefs and those of Christianity. If St. Paul enunciated the principle, "Whatever you eat or drink, do all to the glory of God," Hinduism expounded in minute detail just how this was to be done. There is with them no act without religious significance or that lacks a sanctifying prayer. This extends even to what we should regard as indifferent matters and (if I may be spared from carrying the discussion further) to things that are ordinarily not mentioned at all. Briefly, the whole of life is brought *sub specie aeternitatis.* While there are some details of Hindu custom which may be rather startling, and even shocking to our way of thinking, we might be a good deal less disturbed if we realized upon what ideas they ultimately repose. Therefore while Francis Xavier and his immediate successors reaped an overflowing harvest among the poor, the ignorant, and the despised, nothing whatever was done for the élite, nor was it apparent for a long time how anything could be done to win them.

Then in 1605 there arrived near Madura a group of Jesuits led by a very remarkable man, and they determined to try a new method, one that called for immense learning and a patience as immense. This man, Robert de' Nobili, was a nephew of Cardinal Bellarmine, the celebrated theologian, now canonized and proclaimed a doctor of the Church. When reports reached the Cardinal in Italy of what his nephew was doing, reports that were to a considerable extent fallacious, he was seriously alarmed, thinking at first that too many concessions were being made to Hinduism.

Broadly what happened was this: Nobili, who was already learned in Hindu lore and a notable Sanskrit scholar, arrived wearing the yellow robe of a *sunyasi,* or ascetic, and with a servant going before him bearing a gold-headed staff. He never, as his critics sometimes charged, actually gave out that he was a light-skinned Brahmin from the North, but he did say, when questioned, that he was a rajah from Rome, which was near enough the truth, as he was of noble blood.

At the outset he did not seek to make converts; instead he found a small house for himself, where he could meditate undisturbed and where also he could perfect his knowledge of the sacred books of India. He counted upon the curiosity of people being aroused, so that they would seek him out. To those who did so, he was able to present the Gospel as the completion of Hinduism, and that without straining Christian doctrine. And this, of course, was possible only because he was deeply conversant with Hindu notions.

By degrees he succeeded in making many Brahmin converts. These he allowed to retain some customs of their caste. They might wear the sacred thread and the caste-marks on their foreheads and observe also their dietary regulations; indeed, they might do anything that was not demonstrably at variance with Christianity. To him this meant no more than the preservation of their social rank, and so was indifferent; it did not involve accommodation in essentials.

His learning and that of his co-workers had to be acknowledged by the most learned Brahmin. Other Jesuits, a little later, were Tamil as well as Sanskrit scholars, one of them, Constantine Beschi, producing an epic on the life of St. Joseph which is a recognized classic, though some Tamil critics think it a little too florid in style. I do not know of any literary achievement that parallels this. The Pole Joseph Conrad became a master of English prose, but to be a great poet — especially an epic poet — in a foreign language not learned until manhood is something else again. George Santayana indeed wrote not only first-rate prose but good verse in English, but he was half American and had lived since youth in the United States. Even he says, a little sadly, that some flights of poetry were beyond his capacity, as such things as nursery rhymes had never got into his blood. This does not mean that, even if English had been his mother-tongue, he would have written an epic, for epic poets are extremely rare. But his admission leaves one all the more astounded by Beschi.

The Jesuits attempted to show the Brahmins that Christianity, so far from being inconsistent with Hinduism was, properly understood, its loftier culmination, and this effort proved a greater success than is usually supposed. Undoubtedly it would have won still more sweeping triumphs had it not been that other missionaries in India — one suspects partly because they were envious of the Jesuits — denounced what are called the "Malabar Rites" as a watering-down of Christianity to make it more acceptable to Hinduism. There came from Rome first a condemnation of the Jesuit methods, then a kind of approval which raised such a storm that the Holy See issued an order that all discussion of the matter be dropped, but with it a directive that the Malabar Rites be discontinued. The imposition of silence lasted at least a century, but though I know of no Jesuits [1] now working along the lines initiated by De' Nobili, word has come during the last few years of a couple of Belgian priests in Southern India who have revived these methods (though possibly with some modifications). Moreover, there is a large Benedictine community who dress as *sunyasis* instead of in the habit of their order, and who are close and sympathetic students of Sanskrit and the Indian sacred

---

[1] Recently some Jesuits did attempt something of this sort, but found the Indian hierarchy (many of whose members are of Indian blood), not very favorable. The uneasiness caused was not on account of alleged "accommodation" but was akin to the uneasiness aroused in the minds of the French hierarchy by the priest-workmen.

books. That they must have been successful would seem
to be indicated by word just to hand that a new Benedictine group (of the Cistercian branch) has gone out to
Bangalore, at the invitation of Archbishop Pothacamury,
headed by the Englishman Dom Bede Griffiths,[1] a convert.
He has announced that the "most contemplative people
on earth are soon to have among them the sub-continent's
first strictly contemplative monastery." Except for this,
I do not know Dom Bede's plans, but I am certain that
his projected community will be in the De' Nobili tradition.

A very different sort of experiment to that essayed in
the South of India was made in the North shortly before
De' Nobili, and had it achieved all the results aimed at
could have brought millions of Moslems, and perhaps
also many Indians of other religions, into the Church at
one stroke. This was when the Emperor Akbar, the Great
Mogul (1542–1602), invited Moslems, Hindus and
Parsis, for whom he had established schools where they
could study together without discrimination, to stage a
debate with some Jesuit Fathers. Akbar was a renowned
soldier, driving the Afghans out of Bengal, and annexing
Kabul, Kashmir, Scind and Kandahar, Ajmere, Oudh and
Gwalior and the Gujarat. He was also an administrator
of the utmost justice, and a munificent patron of the arts.
Already he had devised a creed, in which he did not insist on the more rigid tenets of Islam but sought to combine these with the best elements of Hinduism and the
doctrines held by the Parsis. He was therefore receptive
of mind, so the Jesuits, instead of aiming at scoring de-

[1] Father Griffiths, a monk of Prinknash Abbey, recently wrote a bril-
liantly composed autobiography entitled *The Golden String* which, in
part, describes his conversion to Catholicism.

bating points, argued that in Catholicism all the religions of India found their fulfillment. The Great Mogul
admitted the force of much of this, and his prestige was
such that the Jesuits had high hopes that his conversion
would result in an *en masse* conversion of his subjects.
As a first step he gave the Jesuits permission to preach
and baptize without restriction and to found a college
at Agra.

Upon an outbreak of a new war, the Jesuits rode with
him on the campaign, and every night Akbar continued
his stream of questions. They were beginning to think
of him as a new Constantine, when suddenly he died,
and with that there ended the greatest chance that the
Jesuits had in India, or perhaps anywhere in the world.

The episode of Akbar shows that the Jesuits no longer
intended to address themselves to the submerged classes
of the people, but to the rulers and the learned. Even
Francis Xavier, when in Japan, saw that he should go
first to the top men, the king and the nobles, as if they
could be converted, everything else would almost automatically follow. It was with this idea in his mind that
he planned his abortive attempt on China. Though Xavier
failed here, other Jesuits took up his project and, in a
somewhat different fashion, carried it through. Regarding this we have the recent translation from Latin of the
diary of Matteo Ricci (covering the years 1583–1610)
made by Father Louis J. Gallagher. That it is written in
the third person does not diminish its interest to any
great extent, and the method provides Ricci with several
advantages.

He did not, it is true, seek to the same extent as did
De' Nobili, who perhaps stole a leaf from his book, to
show the correspondence between Confucius and Christ.

Perhaps this was in part due to the fact that Confucianism is a philosophy rather than a religion, and Chinese Buddhism was not well developed in its theological ideas. This made the work of Ricci all the easier. In his case he was able to exploit the intense interest taken by the learned Chinese in astronomy and mathematics, subjects in which Ricci was expert, having once been a student under the celebrated astronomer Christopher Clavius.

Nor was this all: the Chinese were fascinated by clocks; as for maps they were astounded by them. They had been convinced that China was the world's "central kingdom," and though they were crestfallen when Ricci demonstrated that they were nothing of the kind, they were also stirred by their new knowledge. It was fortunate that Ricci found so many men in China by whom learning was held in the highest esteem; it was upon this secular learning that he built.

The Chinese nevertheless held, and with their hearts as well as their heads, some concepts that created difficulties to their acceptance of Christianity. One of these was their attitude toward their dead. From one point of view it certainly looks like ancestor worship; from another it could be regarded as either the veneration of saints — in the sense in which great men are honored, or that in which one prays privately to holy souls, even when their canonization is not likely [1] — or even as prayers for

[1] Every Catholic, I suppose, does ask the prayers of his beloved dead, and may regard them as saints. All that the Church forbids is anything like a public cult of such souls until the Church has given the approval of beatification. The prayers, too, of the faithful departed (those who are presumably in purgatory) may be invoked, for if they actually are in purgatory their eventual glory in heaven is assured. Hence the feast of All Saints — the "host that no man can number" seen by St. John in the Apocalypse, which falls on November 1st, is followed the very next day by the feast of All Souls, which is for those still in purgatory.

the souls in purgatory. Some of the ceremonies connected with all this struck the Dominican and Franciscan missionaries when they reached China as rank heathenism, but the Jesuits represented them in another light to the Roman Inquisition and secured their toleration, though eventually the "Chinese Rites" had to be modified.

Again the fact that the chief critics of the Jesuits were found in rival religious orders, makes us a little suspicious of the charges. Ricci could say, quite truly, that the word "sacrifice" is capable of being used in several senses, and that it was a "broad and indefinite sense" that the Chinese had in mind. Father Ricci, when invited to attend one such ceremony, accepted, on the ground that it was no more than an orchestral rehearsal, designed to decide whether the music was appropriate or not. He said: "There was no question of attending a sacrifice."

It was the same with the compendium of Christian doctrine Ricci drew up. In its first version it had to be prepared with the aid of interpreters, but when the Jesuits became more familiar with the language, they saw that it was inadequate and therefore revised it. Ricci then added "citations . . . taken from the ancient Chinese writers; passages which were not merely ornamental, but served to promote the acceptance of this work. . . . It also provided a refutation of all the Chinese religious sects, excepting the one founded on the natural law, as developed by their prince of philosophers, Confucius, and adopted by the sect of the literati." [1]

[1] It is worth remarking that within the last half dozen years two books expounding much the same idea have been published: *Between East and West* by John Wu and *From Confucius to Christ* by Paul K. T. Sih. Both authors are remarkable men. Dr. Wu, at Chiang Kai-Shek's request, translated the New Testament into Chinese and held a position which was not far short of being chief justice of China's Supreme Court. Both men have held ambassadorial office and followed identical

If the Jesuit missionaries in the Orient addressed themselves primarily to the ruling and learned classes, this
was only as a matter of policy; with these won, the masses
could be interested with hardly any effort. Thus the
Jesuits in seventeenth-century China were offered and
accepted mandarin rank, but it should be remembered
that a mandarin was merely a public official and could
only become such by passing a most exacting written
examination, lasting for days, and one open to anybody,
which insured that China's administration would be confined to the learned. Ricci of course did not sit for such
an examination, but he deeply impressed the Chinese with
his scholarship; they saw this in tangible form in his
library, in not a single volume of which could they read
a word. But the printing and binding of the books was
so sumptuous as far to surpass anything produced by the
Chinese themselves. Moreover, they did not fail to notice
that the Jesuit Fathers hired a well-known Chinese
scholar at a good salary to live with them, for they wished
to make themselves conversant with Chinese science.

In short, Ricci and his co-workers utilized science for
the winning of souls to Christ. Ricci was to write: "Who-
ever may think that ethics, physics and mathematics are
unimportant in the work of the Church, is unacquainted
with the taste of the Chinese, who are slow to take a
spiritual potion, unless it be seasoned with an intellectual
flavoring." This, incidentally, is high praise to give the
Chinese; it also tells much about Ricci's own make-up,
the sweetness with which he dedicated his secular learning to spiritual ends.

---

paths in becoming Catholics. What they do is hardly more than to re-
state in Chinese terms the great line of the *Dies Irae: Teste David cum
Sibylla.*

Chinese is said to be perhaps the world's most difficult language. Regarding this Francis Xavier fell under a serious illusion, for when he discovered that the Chinese and the Japanese both use a more or less pictorial script, he imagined that these must at least have a strong resemblance. The truth is that the speaker of one Chinese dialect is not intelligible to the speaker of another. A pleasant apothegm has it that to acquire Chinese one needs a heart of oak, nerves of steel and the years of Methuselah. As for the script, Ricci tells us that it contains about 70,000 to 80,000 symbols, and that when one has mastered about 10,000 of these one "has reached the point in his education where he is ready to begin to write. That is about the least number required for intelligent writing. There probably is no one in the entire kingdom who has mastered all the symbols or has what may be styled a complete ideographic knowledge of the Chinese language." Ricci's own knowledge of Chinese was far from perfect, but his attainments in other branches of knowledge made him accepted by the Chinese as one of the greatest of scholars. He was one of the best of their cartographers, and he entranced the Chinese with his "prisms," in which he analyzed the spectra, and by his clocks. The Chinese have some right to claim that they invented printing before Guttenberg and gunpowder before Roger Bacon, but they did not put them to much practical use; if they were equally taken by some of the things that Ricci thought of as "toys," they were only like most human beings.

Matteo Ricci, as might be expected, had his ups and downs, but his was, upon the whole, a work of steady success, even though he was once accused of a treasonable plot. The fact of the matter is that Ricci did eventually obtain admission to Peking and had an interview with the Emperor himself. Through the imperial favor and the backing of some of the mandarins his work prospered, if not in a spectacular fashion so far as the number of converts he made. If by his death in 1610 there were only 15,000 Chinese Christians, these increased by the middle of the century to 150,000 and to 237,000 by 1664. Unfortunately a bitter controversy arose over what were called "Chinese Rites," [1] and early in the eighteenth century these were prohibited by the Holy See as giving too much accommodation to paganism. Later on, as we know, China was completely closed off to Western influence. But since the mid-nineteenth century the Church in China has made wonderful strides, being eventually largely manned by Chinese priests and even seeing a Chinaman elevated to the cardinalate. Were it not for recent events Catholics in China would be among the most numerous in non-Christian lands. But despite the Communists now in control, we may be sure that the end is not yet.

[1] These permitted the Chinese to take part in certain traditional honors paid to Confucius and their ancestors, to use Chinese designations for the name of God and, as a concession to Chinese etiquette, for the priest to say Mass with head covered.

Eleven

The American Indian

To GIVE AN ACCOUNT of Jesuit missionary work among American Indians would be hardly possible in a short chapter, which indeed must be so very short that it runs the risk of being not much more than a bare enumeration of missionary enterprises. I shall do my best, however, to mention the highlights of what is, in itself, a fascinating story. First, it must be said that even Christopher Columbus took with him Franciscan friars, and some of these were with Cortes in his conquest of Mexico; that Dominicans accompanied Pizarro to Peru; and that Hernando de Soto had in his army a number of priests — most, if not all of them, Franciscans — when he landed in Florida in 1540. The Spanish Crown, and for that matter the *Conquistadores* themselves, were concerned for the conversion as well as the subjugation of the Indians. None of these first missionaries to the New World were Jesuits, for the simple reason that the Society of Jesus was not yet founded; also of course its first efforts were directed towards the Orient.

The Jesuits, however, did not lag in entering this field. In 1566 Pedro Martinez was slain on the coast of Florida by the Indians he was trying to convert; he was the first Jesuit martyr of North America. Only a few years later, in September 1570, during the generalate of St. Francis

Borgia, a Jesuit contingent reached the mouth of the Chesapeake, where at the start the Indians seemed to be friendly enough, but soon turned against them after a few catechumens had been made, and massacred them to the last man. Though Jesuits, even before this, had joined their Franciscan and Dominican confrères in the Southern continent, it was not until the early seventeenth century that Jesuits went to the banks of St. Lawrence, where their first effort proved abortive, partly because those in official charge in Canada, being tainted with Gallicanism and Jansenism (and even Calvinism), put obstacles in their way. Shortly afterward Father Druillettes and others labored among the Abenaki of Maine (at that time claimed by Canada), but in 1724 Sebastian Rasles, who had been the spiritual father of the Indians for thirty years, was killed by Puritan New Englanders, and the Jesuits driven out. Only in Pennsylvania and in Maryland, to which two Jesuits went out in 1634, did they escape the danger of martyrdom. However even in Maryland, which was founded by King Charles I's friend George Calvert, Lord Baltimore — personally a Catholic and one who attempted religious toleration, though Maryland must not be thought of as being, even briefly, a Catholic colony — all Catholics soon were brought under the penal laws passed against them. I leave their story on one side, as it was not primarily that of an enterprise for the benefit of the Indians, but of the whites.

Perhaps before coming to the Indians a preliminary word should be given to the seventeenth-century St. Peter Claver, as his work was in the New World, though he devoted himself not to Indians but to the Negroes of the great slave markets in the West Indies at Cartagena. Unlike the Dominican, Bartolomeo de las Casas, he did

not fight for a cause, but while accepting the fact of
Negro slavery, tried to do what he could to bring physical and spiritual assistance to an unfortunate race. In
fact, he seems to have looked upon these slaves as being
blessed by God. They had been brought from the dark
paganism of Africa to a place where they could become
Christians, and even gain much merit from the patience
with which they accepted their sufferings. Yet he well
understood what those sufferings were, and did all that
was in his power to alleviate them. Therefore, even before he became a priest, he added to the four vows taken
by a Jesuit a fifth: to be for the rest of his life the slave
of the slaves. One would like to go further with the story
of this astonishingly heroic life, but a paragraph will have
to suffice here, if the American Indians are to be dealt
with at all.

Even so, as the work was so very widespread, it would
seem advisable to confine oneself mainly to the Indians
of Canada, to the famous experiment of Paraguay, and
to the later work done in the United States by Father de
Smet. But it should be understood that the omissions
are enormous. For instance, as against one Jesuit college
in Quebec, the Spanish and Portuguese Jesuits established nearly twenty in Latin America, and long, long
before Harvard, there was a Catholic college in Mexico
City. Moreover, while the Jesuits in the North added an
undying luster to their name, their converts were a relatively small body, whereas in Mexico, Peru, Chile, Central America and Brazil, they brought hundreds of thousands into the Church. We are naturally proud of those
whom we call our Jesuit martyrs of the seventeenth century, the majority of whom died on Canadian soil —
nearly all after having undergone hideous tortures —

but there were about eighty Jesuit martyrs in Central and South America, though most of these met a swift and therefore more merciful death. Without forgetting what the missionaries in those parts accomplished, it is impossible, if the restrictions of space be observed, for any attempt to be made to sketch in, however briefly, the whole of the immense Jesuit work in the New World.

The first Jesuit missionary attempt in Canada had to be abandoned, as has been already said; but it was not for very long. In 1625 other Jesuits joined the Recollect friars already working there. Under the command of St. Jean de Brébeuf, they did not take long to press beyond the confines of the garrisoned towns on the St. Lawrence to the settlement of the Hurons, which was northwest of Lake Ontario and on the shore of Georgian Bay, a large indentation of water from Lake Huron. These Hurons were a tribe destined to extinction at the hands of the Iroquois, but seemed savage enough to the Jesuits who went to them. The Fathers were well aware that at any moment a tomahawk might descend, or even that they might be put to the tortures in which the Indians of the Great Lake country territories so delighted. Yet they went serenely on with their work, always under suspicion of practicing maleficent magic, but obtaining a few well-instructed converts. The larger number of those they baptized were the dying or infants; they had to be very careful about this last, because if the child died, baptism (as one of the forms of the Blackrobes' magic) was considered the cause. So also were the Jesuits suspected of causing the various epidemics to which the Indians were so susceptible, or any failure of their few crops.

There were considerable difficulties, too, in holding any communication with these savages, quite apart from the unlikeness of the gutteral Indian speech to the labial French. One was that abstract terms were all but incomprehensible to the Indians, so that for the Sign of the Cross it was necessary to fall back upon: "In the name of our Father, and of His Son, and of their Holy Spirit." Another was that all their verbs were inflected, conjugated in numbers and tenses as in Greek, indeed, with a double conjugation, one direct and the other reciprocal, with sometimes a feminine conjugation as well. The language was richer than French in its complex shades of meaning. Yet even when the elaborate grammar could be mastered, the virtual impossibility of finding a means of conveying abstract ideas remained.

In this connection it might be remarked that the first Christmas carol to be written on this continent, "Jesus is born," was written in 1641 in Huron by one of the Jesuit missionaries, and that at the Indian village just outside of Montreal the Stations of the Cross and even the service books used for responses by the congregation are in Iroquois to this day. It is there that the remnants of a once ferocious tribe still live; and enshrined in their church (which is under the charge of Jesuits) are preserved the bones of Kateri Tekawitha, the "Lily of the Mohawks," in the strong hope of her eventual beatification. She came to holiness, along with others, under the tutelage of the Fathers. These Jesuits found a bestial obscenity of act and speech when they first arrived; but so great a change did they bring about that later other missionaries were often hard put when hearing confessions to discover in the hearts of their converts matter for absolution.

A number of the first missionaries, however, suffered martyrdom and are now canonized. Nor was this ordinary martyrdom, but the acceptance of death that came only after prolonged tortures. The Indians of Western Canada and the northwest corner of what is now the United States had a kind of game that they played with most of their captives. Briefly, this consisted in beginning with stripping the captives stark naked and making them run the gauntlet, from this proceeding to pulling out their fingernails, setting torches to the most sensitive parts of the body, pouring boiling water over their heads, and biting off their fingers, meanwhile dealing out ferocious pleasantries. Those on the opposite side, the tortured, were vastly admired if they could suffer all this without flinching. Even the Indian children took part in the proceedings, for when the prisoners were tied down for the night (for the renewal of their tortures the next day), the small fry, who were learning their first lessons in cruelty, used to throw live coals over the bodies stretched on the ground. Death came, as a final mercy, only after everything else that the savages could think of had been done.

Parkman was the earliest of the Jesuits' historians — if we except John Gilmary Shea, for their activities form only a small part of the latter's monumental *History of the Catholic Church in the United States*. More recently excellent lives of Brébeuf and Isaac Jogues have been written by Father Francis X. Talbot, and these seem to be definitive. Parkman wrote, after all, with Puritan prejudices and Shea is incomplete, even if his *History* is always to be held in honor as glorious pioneering.

Brébeuf himself suffered a hideous martyrdom, along with others of the Fathers, but it was in Canada; I will go on to a few of the martyrs made from his group on the soil of the present United States. Isaac Jogues and two laymen who were acting as assistants to the Jesuits were captured by the Iroquois on the St. Lawrence, almost within sight of Three Rivers. They were brought the whole length of Lake Champlain into upper New York State, made to undergo the usual tortures but, for the moment, their lives were spared. Indeed, Jogues was "adopted" by an Indian family, whom he served as a slave as best he could with badly mutilated hands.

This was in an encampment about forty miles northwest of the present Albany, where the Dutch had a trading-station and fort. At last Jogues managed to escape to them, and they kept him carefully hidden until he could be conveyed down the Hudson in a small ship, to what is known today as New York. From this port he eventually managed to make his way to the Jesuit college at Rennes in Brittany. There he arrived on Christmas Day, 1642, and was questioned as to whether he knew anything about what had happened to Père Jogues, of whom the last heard was that he had been captured by the Indians. Stretching out his mangled hands, the tattered stranger replied, "I am Jogues."

The Pope gave him special permission to offer Mass, despite mutilations that would ordinarily have made this impossible. Then Jogues begged to be allowed to return to the fierce Iroquois and was accredited by the governor of Quebec as his ambassador to the Indians. As such he was received with fitting honor and was so encouraged that he soon returned to Quebec bearing proposals which it was hoped would end the bloody feud between the Hurons and the "Five Nations." Then he went back to his former captors in his capacity as priest, but by this time their suspicions had revived and they looked upon him as one who practiced a peculiarly baleful form of magic. Though at the Indian councils not all concurred, a young brave took it upon himself to split Jogues' head with a tomahawk. One of the lay assistants captured with him the previous year, and whom he had secretly received as a member of the Company of Jesus as they made their way down Lake Champlain, had long since been put to death. He is now canonized as St. René Goupil.

Jogues' treatment was typical of what had to be faced by the Jesuit missionaries. Yet it never deterred them from going far afield, despite all dangers. Thus Père Marquette, accompanied by Joliet, a layman, traversed the length of the Mississippi with five Indians in a couple of birchbark canoes. On May 17, 1673, when they started, Marquette wrote: "The joy that we felt at being selected for this expedition animated our courage, and rendered the labors of paddling from morning to night agreeable to us. . . . And because we were going to seek unknown countries, we took every precaution in our power, so that if our undertaking were hazardous, it should not be foolhardy." It was largely because of Marquette's careful observation that Delisle was able to make the most beautifully detailed map of the whole Mississippi Valley which was included in the 1728 edition of Garcilasso de la Vega. The Great River had of course been first discovered in 1541 by Hernando de Soto, but not much was known about it until Père Marquette's explorations.

Similarly, and about the same time as Marquette's expedition, Eusebio Kino, a Tyrolese Jesuit working in Mexico, demonstrated that the peninsula of Lower California was not an island, as had hitherto been supposed, but was attached to the mainland. This led to an establishment of Jesuit missions there, which lasted until all

members of the order were unceremoniously bundled out
of every part of the Spanish dominions.

Even in Mexico — except perhaps for the officials in
Mexico City — life was not very comfortable, though the
Indians had been broken too thoroughly by Cortes to
rise, and, in the case of some of their chiefs, became assimilated to Spanish life, a few of them even receiving
Spanish titles. Yet there were outlying parts of the Spanish and Portuguese possessions in South America, and
even in Mexico, in which the enemies of the Jesuits pic-
tured wholly fabulous gold and silver mines, worked by
the natives under the direction of the Fathers. Even in remote and bare Lower California it was imagined that
the Fathers were enriching themselves by means of pearl
fisheries. Wild stories of this sort did much to prepare
for the wholesale ejection of the Jesuits by King
Charles III in 1767, though when that occurred it is
hardly necessary to say that no signs of mines or any
kind of pearl fisheries were found.

There did exist, however, some material wealth of
another kind, though the Jesuits themselves did not obtain any particle of it, and wished for none. This was in
Paraguay, which has probably never been better described for us than by Cunninghame Graham as "a Lost
Utopia" — the title for his book on the subject. There, in
the interior of South America, the Jesuit missionaries
led their converts deeper and deeper into the forests so
as to escape the "mamelukes," or slave-traders, who used
Saõ Paulo as their headquarters. A large tract was at last
found between rivers which gave them some protection,
though the time came when these "Reductions," as they
were called, had to raise armed forces for self-defense,
and even to make cannon.

These cannon consisted of no more than strips of wood, bound together with hoops, as a cask is, and hardly more effective, as they were able to fire only a few small balls of stone — not very accurately — before falling to pieces. However, they and the Indian armies served to put some fear into the slave-raiders. One of the Indian chiefs was put in military command and this was distorted to the myth that one of the Jesuits, under the name of Nicholas, was king in Paraguay.

So far from these Indians being exploited, they were the only ones of their people who possessed any land, either as individuals or in common. The Jesuits, however, were obliged somehow to solve the problem of inducing a naturally lazy people to do the work in the fields to which the Indians were so disinclined. The difficulty was met through their love of music. Accordingly the day was organized on a musical basis, the people of the Reductions marching out to work with bands playing and returning in the same way. Under this system they prospered in a way as had never entered their dreams, but the Fathers got nothing, except the satisfaction of serving God.

The Indians were also fond of dramatic representations; of this fact advantage was taken, as this was an excellent way for the Jesuits to keep their flocks amused and out of mischief. Though the Indians, with few exceptions, remained illiterate, this does not mean that they did not acquire some culture along other lines. The ruins of their churches, which may still be seen, show of what the Indian builders were capable under the direction of the Fathers. These churches are larger and much more elaborate than anything the Franciscan missionaries achieved a little later in what is now the State of California. The simplicity of the Californian churches has been greatly — in my estimation, too greatly — admired. Their lines are, in fact, very good, but even this was to some extent due to the fact that the Franciscans had to condition their work to adobe, which perforce could not rise to anything elaborate; and the Californian Indians, whose intelligence was not very high, were not capable of anything more. The Franciscans should be given the credit of gauging quite correctly just how much they might extract from their neophytes, but we know from the churches they erected in Mexico, which Junípero Serra himself erected where skilled masons were available, that the Californian style was accepted only as the best he could hope for, and is not to be taken as what he preferred. In that age of the baroque — for that style still held its ground — the Jesuits gave their taste fuller reign. More important, in Paraguay, where the missionaries were not interfered with at every turn by rule-of-thumb officialdom, and where the system of Reductions removed most of the danger from slave-raiders, it was possible to bring the Indians to a higher degree of civilization than was possible in California.

This should not be taken as belittling Junípero Serra, who did all that could be done under the circumstances, and then a bit more. But the Jesuits in Paraguay and their converts enjoyed more advantages; to those that have already been mentioned should be added that in the Reductions the whites were always kept from contact with the Indians. In some instances the savages of California may have derived benefit from contact with the soldiers, or the handful of Spanish workmen employed by the missions, but more usually this was likely to be demoralizing. If the work in the Reductions ended in ejec-

tion and eventually was utterly destroyed, this was because of the policy adopted by both the Portuguese and
Spanish governments. As it is, the Reductions of Paraguay must be regarded as the most successful experiment
of its kind ever attempted.

In spite of a vast wrong of this sort done to the Indians
themselves — who suffered mainly because of the blow
that was struck against the Jesuits in the late eighteenth
century by Portugal and Spain — it is open to observation that the Latin countries of South and Central
America have dealt with the Indians in a better fashion
than has been true of the "Anglo-Saxon" Northern continent. From what I have heard I would gather that the
Latin dominions often reduced their Indian population
to virtual peonage, but the Portuguese and Spaniards
freely married Indian women, and in not a few cases
their offspring rose to positions of wealth and high administrative power, whereas the New Englander, and
still more the frontiersman, operated on the principle
that "the only good Indian is a dead Indian." In this they
did have some justification, as they often had to suffer
from the depredations of the red men.

It may be argued that the North American Indians did
not "own," in our sense of the term, the wide tracts they
needed for hunting and trapping. Even so, all too commonly faith was not kept with them, and a favorite trick
was to make them so drunk that they had no idea what
concessions they were making. The Indians were pushed
further and further West until there was nowhere for
them to go except into the Indian reservations. There
most of them still remain, not as in a concentration camp
but choosing to remain among their kind, gloomily
meditating upon their ancient way of life, which they

are convinced is superior to that of the whites. Eventually
— though this is not likely to be in the foreseeable future
— it is to be expected that all will be assimilated as ordinary Americans, for a trickle in that direction is already
going on. When complete fusion occurs the mass of
white Americans may be able to pardon themselves for
their treatment of the aboriginal race.

Yet even in frontier days in North America the Indians
found those who wished to befriend them. One was the
ex-Sulpician Bishop Simon Bruté; another was Mother
Philippine Duchesne, of the Religious of the Sacred
Heart, who is now beatified. She, in fact, came to America
with the specific intention of working among the Indians,
and although she was not able to carry out her ambition
until old age, she and her nuns did accomplish a great
deal of good among them. There should also be recorded
the names of the John Baptist Miège, appointed bishop
of the Indian territory in 1850, and of Gailland, Point and
Hoecken, all of them Jesuits, though not the only Jesuits
who dedicated themselves to this field of labor. In
Hoecken's mouth it was said that Potawattomi sounded
as mellifluous and liquid as the softest Greek or Italian.

The most illustrious of all these Jesuit missionaries was
the Belgian, Peter de Smet. Working among the tribes of
the Rocky Mountain area and west to the Coast of
Oregon, he had great influence among the Flatheads, the
Nez Percés and other tribes and was able to pacify the
most warlike among them, at one time going alone into a
camp of five thousand hostile Sioux to get them to accept a
treaty of peace. He often defended the Indian cause before the American government in Washington, and in
their behalf he traveled constantly not only over the
United States but crossed the ocean nineteen times, beg-

ging aid for them from Pope Pius IX, various European monarchs, and before audiences of the humble as well as the great. On his constant journeys for the raising of funds, he was everywhere received with honor by the most highly placed people of his day, who did not in the least mind that their visitor was attired in a rusty frock coat, from which a button or two was usually missing. Among his Indians, he himself became an Indian, learning how to attend twenty feasts sometimes in a single day (he was luckily corpulent), as a refusal of any invitation was likely to give some offense. He found even the flesh of a dog delicious, or professed to. He was the only white man the Indians could trust, for only he never talked with "a double tongue." Since his day there have been many devoted missionaries to the Indians, drawn from many orders of priests as well as Sisters; but there has never been more than one De Smet. That there should have been even one is more than the world deserves.

Twelve

The Suppression

STARTLING as was the Papal suppression of the
Society of Jesus in 1773, it was an act perfectly within the
rightful powers of the Holy See. That is, if one looks at
the matter in the abstract, prescinding from all the historical circumstances that led up to it. Religious communities in the past had every now and then been
obliged to suffer from a trial of this sort, especially when
it happened that they had rather obviously exhausted
their usefulness. But such religious communities had almost always been small and their extinction was hardly
noticed, perhaps giving even to those suppressed some
degree of relief. However, the Templars could hardly be
described as small and were very wealthy, but though
they were assuredly innocent of most of the things with
which they were charged even if abuses had occurred,
the Knights Templars since the end of the Crusades had
no real excuse for being. Pope Clement V, in conjunction
with King Philip the Fair, dealt with them in France and
Henry VIII, in a milder fashion, did the same in England more than two hundred years later. But the Templars are not a real parallel, as they were obsolete,
whereas the Jesuits in 1773 were doing a great work for
the Church, and were at the height of their prosperity.

They fell because they had created so many enemies,

and some Jesuits suggest, with what wears the appearance of over facility, that they were hated as they were because of the vow of obedience they took to the Pope. That this may have had something to do with the matter is likely enough but is far from being an adequate explanation. In addition, the Jesuits as a group were considered by many to have rather too much *esprit de corps*. This is an excellent thing within due bounds, and does much for the regiment and the school as well as the religious order. But while it is hard, if not impossible, to say just when it becomes excessive, a hair's breadth may make it look like arrogance. Yet the most intense pride in the group may exist in a member who is personally quite humble; if so, it does not do much to make his *esprit de corps* acceptable, should other people consider that it is being carried too far.

One must choose one's words carefully: for practical purposes it is not necessary that the characteristic mentioned should actually exist; it is quite enough that it be imagined to exist. We all know how a general impression can be easily (and altogether unconsciously) created by a miniscule minority, with most unfortunate results. It must be evident from the pages of this book that the Society had many valid reasons for being proud of its achievements. Nevertheless, it is possible that, on occasion, indiscreet Jesuits mentioned too often, and with too much complacency, their distinguished men, the long and intensive training the Society demands, or even (in extreme instances) may have suggested that the religious life as lived by them was of a higher character than that reached by similar institutes. Men being constituted as they are, this would be enough.

Then we must always allow for the rivalry that some-

times exists between groups of religious. As we have
seen earlier, the Jesuits and the Dominicans had had
rather bitter theological disagreements. That these were
frequently over minor questions makes little difference;
what counted was the bitterness. And the Franciscans
had taken much the same line as the Dominicans about
the "Malabar Rites" and the "Chinese Rites," calling them
"accommodation," that is, a willingness to permit pagans
to retain customs that were at variance with Christianity.

In European countries at that time a point of prestige
was also involved. The Jesuits had established so many
excellent schools and colleges that they seemed almost
to have acquired a preserve in the education of the upper classes. And it may be that they did supply more than
their quota of royal confessors. However scrupulous these
confessors were to keep strictly within the bounds of
their spiritual office, it is easy to see how they might be
suspected of meddling in purely political concerns. Again,
it is not so much what was really true that counted but
what was imagined. But it is not impossible that a
royal confessor here and there may have occasionally
made a not quite proper use of his position.

Other complications of the issue — primarily in France
but to some extent in other countries — arose over the
controversies concerning Gallicanism and Jansenism.
Gallicanism may be roughly described as the doctrine of
the "divine right of kings" in its French form.[1] When

[1] Though Gallicanism, in its old French form, no longer exists, a
footnote about it might be called for here. While the germs of it had
existed before, it was formulated in a document issued by the French
clergy in 1628. According to this, St. Peter and his successors had no
authority in temporal affairs over princes; the deposing power of the
Pope was denied; and the Councils of the Church ranked above the
Pope. It lingered on until the French Revolution, though it did now
and then show its head in England, and even Ireland still later. It is no

James I of England advanced his theory of royal
authority and the superiority of the State over the
Church, he attempted to refute the great theologian
Bellarmine, and Bellarmine and other Jesuits were
equally opposed to Gallicanism, something made a good
deal less easy for them by the fact that the Papacy had
conferred upon the kings of Spain wide rights of ecclesiastical appointment. What we should never forget is
that secular authorities are always tempted to try and
use the Church as a department of government. As for
Jansenism, which was a kind of Catholic Calvinism,
though it was decisively condemned by the Holy See and
has long since been dead as a positive doctrine, it still
exists as a miasma upon which it is usually hard to lay a
finger, but which, being an impalpable infection, retains
some of its corrupting power. That the Jesuits had so
vigorously opposed both these forces, created enemies
for them, often all the more dangerous because these
enemies were capable of acting with such a bland air
of innocence.

Hardly any readers now exist for Bishop Jansenius
(who was always hardly readable) or for his popularizers
Jean du Vergier de Huranne (better known as the Abbé
of Saint-Cyran, the title of his benefice) or the brilliant
but shifty Antoine Arnauld; but everybody has heard of
Port-Royal, and many suppose that those gathered
around that center represent Catholicism at its best,
mainly because of the shining name of Blaise Pascal. His
Pensées is one of the great books of French literature, and
his *Provincial Letters,* though they have lost most of their

---

longer openly professed, except by the so-called Old Catholics; but it
remains a potential danger, as it may be revived in some new form,
though this does not appear likely.

controversial force, are still a classic of French prose. As he was also a man of lofty and charming character, despite a few aberrations, and sufficiently orthodox despite his relations with the Jansenists, his attack on the Jesuits in the *Provincial Letters* is sometimes given more weight than it deserves. If this book was placed upon the Index, so was many another book written by a good Catholic. If that is true today, it was even more true during the eighteenth century.

Yet even in the eighteenth century other enemies of the Jesuits were obliged to cease taking Pascal's charges very seriously. In any event the man's contacts with Jansenism were peripheral; he wrote as he did largely because his Jansenist friends pumped him full of not very accurate information about the Jesuit tendency to be lax as confessors. Voltaire himself, who was assuredly no friend to the Jesuits, admitted the untenability of Pascal's thesis when he wrote: "The extravagant opinions of particular Spanish and Flemish Jesuits were skilfully attributed to the whole Society of Jesus. Similar material could have been unearthed from the works of Dominican and Franciscan casuists, but it was only done in the case of the Jesuits. These *Letters* endeavored to prove that the object of the Jesuits was to pervert the morals of humanity — an object which has never dominated any sect or organization nor can ever do so."

It can be shown fairly conclusively that Pascal had never really studied the works of Escobar, who is his showpiece of horror, though no doubt Pascal had read certain passages to which his Jansenist friends drew his attention, and had dipped hurriedly and carelessly into Escobar here and there. Escobar was a theologian of note, though the article on him in the *Catholic Encyclopedia* observes that there are things in his writing that deserve some censure. This merely repeats in a more moderate form Voltaire's objection: it is grossly unfair to make all the members of a group of more than 20,000 men responsible for the more or less eccentric views that happen to be held by one of their members.

Pascal's attack has given a sinister connotation to the very word "casuistry." But it must be remembered that — quite apart from what a confessor may say to his penitent — any tribunal that has to deliver judgments on moral matters has to bear in mind special circumstances that now and then enter into the case. It is often so in our law courts, not to mention that doctors and even businessmen are sometimes obliged to practice a form of casuistry, if a just decision is to be reached with regard to a particular matter. There are necessarily limits to all this: rules have to be followed; it is only that *sometimes* there are factors that oblige an exception to be made in particular cases. A rigidity that would never admit such exceptions would be inhuman. Pascal is more than a bit absurd when he sees "the whole system of Christian ethics undermined by such a set of monstrous principles." Although Pascal is supposed to have won his battle against the Jesuits, his *Provincial Letters* are seldom, and the works of Escobar virtually never, read.

Pascal was of course promptly answered, to which his reply was that he never denied that the Jesuits were able to trot out some moral theologians who were more strict than the lax Escobar. The conclusive answer is that Pope Innocent XI in 1679 condemned laxism, just as Alexander VIII condemned rigorism in 1690. Not only Jesuits but all Catholic priests are carefully trained as to how to deal with doubtful cases that occasionally — only very occasionally — occur.

The gist of Pascal's charges is to be found in Macaulay,

whose astonishing textual memory this time slipped a bit but which, in slipping, enabled Macaulay to state what he thought he remembered Pascal to have said, and perhaps for that very reason enabled him to make his point all the more effectively. Macaulay wrote: "The gay cavalier who had run his rival through the body, the frail beauty who had forgotten her marriage vow, found in the Jesuit an easy well-bred man of the world, who knew how to make allowances for the little irregularities of people of fashion. The confessor was strict or lax, according to the temper of the penitent. The first object was to drive no person out of the Church. Since there were bad people, it was better that they should be bad Catholics than bad Protestants." The passage is most amusing but is of course even more misleading than Pascal ever was. "People of fashion" do not get greater leniency from their confessors than do others, and the last couple of Macaulay's comments are wholly false, for the confessor in his box sits as the representative of Christ Himself, to whom he will have to render an account on the Judgment Day. The purpose of what is called casuistry — it might be better described as the weighing of all factors with the most just and delicate discrimination — is of course not to drive people out of the Church by over-severity but to save souls by the sacrament of penance.[1]

Pascal, fine character as he was, had every intention of being honest. The same cannot be said of some other

[1] I know of nobody who has been driven out of the Church in this way, though I know scores who have dropped the practice of their religion over some matter such as the confessor's not agreeing (how *can* he agree?) that the practice of unlawful birth-control is harmless, or that a valid marriage may be contracted if a previous bond still exists. There are, however, other matters concerning which the penitent, if refused absolution by one confessor, is free to lay his cause for judgment before another.

critics of the Jesuits, many of whom are embittered ex-
Jesuits, whose intention is pretty plainly the evening of
scores with their former confrères. Of these undoubtedly
the most malicious and mendacious was the seventeenth-
century author (at first anonymous) of the *Monita
Secreta*. This was written by the Polish Jerome
Zahorowski who had been expelled from the order and
it was alleged to reveal the secret instructions directing
the Jesuit machinations. For many years it had been
circulated throughout Europe and reprinted in various
languages; it did much damage because it purported to
come "straight from the horse's mouth," although it has
always been held in contempt by serious historians as a
palpable forgery and even by such enemies of the Jesuits
as Arnauld, the Jansenist. After the suppression of the
Society, their enemies ransacked the Jesuit archives
from top to bottom but did not find the tiniest trace of
"secret instructions." And the only man who may be considered to be one of those "secret Jesuits" we have heard
so much about was St. Francis Borgia; this was because
he was given permission after he had entered the order to
appear before the world in his former style of the Duke
of Gandia until he had arranged all his affairs and in particular had seen to the marriage of several of his numerous children. But of course Zahorowski made more
charges than that, though all of them at best were only
half-truths distorted by spite.

To return to the eighteenth century: to the causes of
the animosity toward the Jesuits that have been in-
stanced, another must be added: the enmity felt by the
rationalist "philosophers" of the Enlightenment. I am not
prepared to say what factor was decisive, and probably
none by itself could have achieved what happened. There

were good people who were opposed to the Jesuits, but usually for a reason that was not good at all, as it sprang from rivalry or envy. Many of the "philosophers" were probably decent fellows in their way; they merely happened to believe that Deism was preferable to Catholicism and that if only the Jesuit organization could be broken up, the doctrines of Christianity would fall. "*Ecrasez l'infâme*" was the war cry furnished them by Voltaire. As the majority of politicians were also "philosophers," a formidable opposition was provided.

Shortly before the Papal suppression of the Society of Jesus in 1773, Portugal, France and Spain ejected all the Jesuits in their dominions. The whole body consisted of over 23,000 men, of whom perhaps the largest contingent worked in France, but with several other thousands who were missionaries in the possessions of the other countries. All this was a preliminary to the final catastrophe, which it was taken for granted would prove fatal.

The prime mover in the matter was Sebastian José Carvalho, better known as the Marquis of Pombal, who was in complete control of Portugal and its king and was consumed by an insensate hatred of the Society; he also was very adroit in the wires he pulled in Spain and France. Pombal was a boorish fellow of enormous physical strength and, after he obtained power, displayed a ferocious cruelty toward many members of the nobility as well as implacable animosity toward the Jesuits. He transformed the Inquisition into a department of state, a clever move, as it enabled him to invest his misdeeds with a kind of religious sanction. In 1750 he struck against the Jesuits and kept to his task until every one of them had been driven out of the Portuguese dominions, keeping some in underground dungeons, though most found a haven in the Papal states from which they could only ruefully contemplate the ruin of their work.

France came next. From that country the Jesuits were expelled, except for such as were allowed to remain to conduct some of their colleges, but only as secular priests under the control of a priest used as the instrument of the government. This much was allowed only because it would have been senseless to abandon the fine college buildings and impossible to staff them with lay teachers who, if they could have been secured, would have had to receive salaries. In France the King, Louis XV, was personally well disposed toward the order, and he managed to stave off the blow for several years, despite the pressure that was put upon him. The Duc de Choiseul, his chief minister, might not have succeeded in ousting them had it not been that the Jesuit who was the King's confessor over and over again refused to give absolution to La Pompadour, the royal mistress, who hankered to appear before the public as a respectable woman.

It may be that another factor operated still more, for nobody likes to lose money, least of all Frenchmen. It so happened that the local superior in the island of Martinique in the West Indies, a Jesuit named La Valette, had most injudiciously and contrary to canon law and the Constitutions of the Society, mixed himself up in business undertakings. His motives were good, for he only wished to help the planters, deriving no profit for himself and the Jesuits. All went well until, right in the middle of the Seven Years' War, when the finances of France were at a low ebb, several ships that were being used by La Valette were lost at sea. When the creditors of La Valette demanded their money, he was naturally quite unable to pay.

The Jesuit authorities in France had once or twice before covered La Valette's losses, but these had been on a small scale (though his business ventures were still impermissible); it was, however, a very different matter when the amount lost was represented as 4,500,000 livres, though La Valette declared it really did not come to much more than half that. The French Assistancy was able to say that, quite apart from the exaggerations of the creditors, the superior at Martinique had no authority to act as a private banker, whatever his benevolent intentions, and La Valette's superiors in France had not been informed as to what had been going on and were unable to exercise effective control over a man 4,000 miles away. Moreover, according to Church law, which the State recognized, each house, province or mission was a separate legal entity so far as finances were concerned. These arguments proved unavailing, for in the lawsuit that was brought the decision went against the Society.

It would have been better for the French Fathers if they had assumed the debt, whatever its legality; instead they made the disastrous mistake of appealing the case to the Parlement. The heads of the order should have understood that this body contained a number of Jansenists, and perhaps even more free-thinking "philosophers," and also a number of Gallican legalists who were equally as bitter. These politicians banded together against the common enemy. Not only did they rule against the Jesuits on the Martinique issue but they more or less plausibly suggested that the Society had vast hoards cached away somewhere or other. Accordingly they seized this opportunity for a production of all documents in the Jesuit archives; all French subjects were prohibited from entering the Society; twenty-four Jesuit books were condemned to be burned by the public hangman; Jesuits were debarred from teaching theology; and attendance was forbidden at Jesuit schools. At the King's instance the decree was suspended for a year, but the Parlement conceded nothing, except that Jesuits might teach, though only under the supervision of a secular priest of the kind the government approved.

Spain acted almost simultaneously, again largely because of Pombal's instigation, though its own more prominent ministers were "philosophers" and did not need much urging. The King, Charles III, was not very intelligent; indeed, if one had to judge from the portrait Goya made of him, he was close to being a half-wit. But he seems to have been persuaded that the Jesuits were implicated in a plot against his life, though this was so preposterous that he made a mystery of the whole thing, writing to tell the Pope that his reasons were "hidden in his heart," which can only mean that they would not bear the light of day. Yet his decree went out: on April 2, 1767, all the Fathers and Brothers of the Society in his dominions were to be herded toward waiting ships, being permitted to carry away with them only a change of clothes and their breviaries. The local officers were to see that the royal order was carried out under pain of death. However old or sick any Jesuit was made no difference, or even if he had to be carried out because he was dying; all had to go on April 2nd. In this way Spain got rid at a stroke of over 2,600 Jesuits. As the Papal States were already overcrowded, these found shelter in Corsica.

The peninsula of Lower California provides an instructive as well as rather amusing light on the matter. There the Franciscans, under Junípero Serra, were sent to replace the Jesuits. The band of soldiers who accompanied them had among their duties the discovering of the secret hoards of pearls supposed to have been amassed. The oysters of those waters did in fact contain pearls, but all were so small as to have no value! Something of the same thing had happened already in Paraguay when the Portuguese authorities searched high and low for the mines that had been worked by the Indians supposedly for the benefit of the Fathers — and of course found nothing whatever. The myth of Jesuit wealth had inflamed the cupidity of the secular authorities; it is perhaps the most beautiful example of a mare's nest that has ever been known.

The ejection of the Jesuits was stupid in another way. Spain and Portugal had a great many other missionaries available, yet still could hardly afford to get rid of the Jesuits. Missionaries were so fully acknowledged to be of service to the secular officials that Spain at one time had spent as much upon maintaining them as upon its colonial armies. In fact the armies could be small — a mere police force — and therefore cost little precisely because it was conceded that the priest did more than the soldier, as he civilized as well as Christianized. The "peaceful conquest" conducted by the missionaries was much more economical than that carried out by large numbers of soldiers, as they could not do much more than cow the savages. However, as the peaceful conquest had by this time achieved its results, the government believed that it could get along with fewer priests; therefore the Jesuits were unceremoniously bundled out. The official mind was bemused not only with mythical mines and pearl-fisheries but with chimerical theories.

All this was bad enough, but the worst was still to

come. Nothing could content the enemies of the Jesuits
except that the entire Society be suppressed by the Pope.
Their grand opportunity arrived when, upon the death
of Clement XIII, a new Pope was elected as Clement XIV. This was Cardinal Ganganelli, who had once
been described as a Jesuit in the Franciscan habit and
was assuredly far from being an enemy of the Society.
The report is utterly untrue that in the conclave that
elected him he gave any promise, either in writing or
orally, that he would do anything that might be considered in repayment for his election, for this of course
would have been invalidating simony. But the Bourbon
monarchies were able to exercise an effective power of
veto, and they made it quite clear which candidates they
considered acceptable. Ganganelli was elected because
it came to be decided that he was the candidate most
likely to do what was wanted with regard to the Jesuits.

No sooner had he been elected to the throne of St.
Peter than the Bourbon monarchs ganged up on him. Left
to himself, he would never have acted as he eventually
did, but the constant pressure eventually proved too
much for him. The Pope could not deny that the Society
of Jesus had become obnoxious in the eyes of the most
powerful Christian kings of that time, and though he
did his best to allay the tumult that was raging, he was
able to accomplish nothing. At last he yielded to the argument that the only way of obtaining peace in the Christian world was to suppress the Jesuits altogether, and
therefore in 1773 he issued his brief *Dominus ac Redemptor;* it marked the triumph of the Society's enemies.

Even so, these enemies were not quite content. What
the Pope had signed was a brief, not a bull, which meant
that it could be more easily abrogated by one of his

successors. Moreover, outright condemnation was missing; the measure taken was indicated only as taken for the restoration of peace, and few popes would have been able to resist so laudable an object. A number of old controversies were cited, a number of complaints that had been brought against the Jesuits, but the Pope protested his own love for them. Though he naturally did not say this, the real reason for what happened was that Clement XIV was not able to cope with those who were supposed to be Christian kings. Yet even in reluctantly yielding, he did what he could to protect from further oppression or acrimonious controversy those who from that moment had to be considered ex-Jesuits. Possibly he was already lifting his eyes to distant horizons, hoping for a calmer world in which the Jesuits could return to their work in peace.

Thirteen

The Rump of the Society

It was generally supposed that the Pope's brief meant that the Society of Jesus was completely ended. And in most countries, all the countries in fact in which Jesuits had been numerous, such was the effect of the *Dominus ac Redemptor*, at least for nearly forty years. But though ways were devised by which a few Jesuits could hold together under new titles — providing, it was hoped, a nucleus for the restoration for which Jesuits everywhere never ceased to pray — these were not very effective.

However, the Society of Jesus in an extremely attenuated form found two countries in which it could continue to function with perfect legality. Two of the monarchs of Europe, neither of them Catholic and one of them forthright in his professions of unbelief, simply refused to allow the Pope's brief to be published in their domains. That it was not published meant, for practical purposes, that it had no force there, even that it did not exist. Under canon law Jesuits not only might continue in these places, but they were not free to disband even of their own volition, and they remained as strictly bound as ever by the vows they had taken in happier years.

One of these countries was Prussia, ruled by Frederick the Great; the other was Russia, ruled by Catherine the

Great. That they of all people came forward as the protectors of the Jesuits presents an aspect that is decidedly comical. Frederick was the friend and patron of Voltaire, who had lived a considerable time at his court, and Voltaire was among the arch foes of the Jesuits. Yet for good reasons of his own the King wanted to have Jesuits in his dominions.

Their other protector had eclipsed a previous empress, Messalina, in profligacy, taking one paramour after another in incredible profusion. But she, like Frederick, was a person of remarkable intelligence, so much so that she may be considered as the only "intellectual" who has ever sat upon the Russian throne. When Catholic Poland was made part of her empire, she had more Jesuits under her sway than had Frederick (though he also had shared in the partition of Poland), so that Russia became the main center from which the Society operated in its greatly truncated form.

Out of deference to the Holy Father, the superior in Russia refrained from styling himself the General of the Jesuits, though that is what, in fact, he really was. And Catherine was punctilious about observing all diplomatic courtesies. The Society therefore received word from the Holy See that its existence was recognized, and, as the years went by, other indications arrived showing that the Pope was not at all displeased, from which it was rightly inferred that there was solid ground for hoping for eventual abrogation of the brief of 1773. The situation, while still far from satisfactory, was at least workable and canonically perfectly valid.

The two non-Catholic monarchs were straightforward, which is much more than can be said of the Most Christian King and the Most Catholic King (not to mention the wretched creature under the thumb of Pombal); also they were vastly better endowed in gray matter. They candidly said that they wished to obtain an education for their upper classes in an economical fashion. Moreover, they knew that the Jesuits were not only more economical than salaried teachers, even if they could have obtained a sufficient supply of these, but much more efficient. They refused to throw away the good they had in their hands, especially as, not being Catholics, they were not obliged to take any positive action, but merely to refrain from publishing the Pope's brief.

On the other hand, the countries of Western Europe that were governed by Catholic monarchs, but dominated by politicians of little or no faith, had no intention of losing what they had obtained from the Pope after a long struggle. But even in France where the high standard of education (mainly reached because of the many excellent Jesuit colleges there) made it possible to obtain good teachers, these teachers expected to be well paid. For this reason the Jesuits were permitted to remain in their colleges, though not as Jesuits, but only as men willing to give instruction gratis under the direction of some tool picked by those in power.

It would have been enormously costly to have provided the salaries of laymen or secular priests out of State funds. Already there were murmurs about over-taxation, so that it was considered risky, if not suicidal, to provide for such teachers out of new taxes. The Revolution was not far away, as the wiser sort of men discerned. Therefore the difficulty was circumvented by a subterfuge which, however, did not permit the Jesuits to function in their true character: the Society remained strictly suppressed, which was only in accordance — as the tender conscience of the pious might reflect—with the Pope's brief.

The ex-Jesuits themselves were punctilious in their obedience to the brief of 1773; they were also cautious in what they did or said, because official animosity might have brought new troubles upon them. They had taken a vow of obedience to the Pope, and that vow they intended to keep with the utmost exactness. It is without precedent that a well-organized group of 23,000 men should have submitted at once and without complaint to an edict that destroyed their very existence. The decree of Clement XIV was infinitely worse than their ejection from the domains of Portugal, France and Spain, for whereas they had been merely thrown out of parts of the world—large parts, and in which they had been doing valuable work—the Pope suppressed the entire Society everywhere, except such fragments as survived in Prussia and Russia. Yet they obeyed, though none of them had ever imagined that the obedience they had vowed would have to be exercised in this way.

Here Father James J. Daly has a searching question to ask. After noting that literature finds its inspiration in great tragedy, he inquires: "Where are the memoirs, the journals, the ruck of books and pamphlets which tragedy of world-wide dimensions usually leaves in its wake? . . . Why did not the stricken Jesuits speak out? They were not inarticulate: as a body they were the most articulate men of the time. They were not unlettered Acadians, who, like the poor and unlettered of every age, had to bear injustice and tyranny with pathetic endurance." They could have found plenty to say, but said nothing whatever. One can only admire their astounding patience and obedience.

It should again be pointed out that ejection on the part of the secular governments, and even Papal suppression, brought nothing damaging to light from the Jesuit archives. In 1773 in Rome itself seals were set by soldiers on all the places where the Society kept its documents, and the General and his assistants cast (however only briefly) into jail, though they could not be charged with any crime. That they had been bitterly assailed on various grounds had long been public property, but those who ransacked their archives from top to bottom could produce nothing worse than the merest trivialities.

One would suppose that this would have given the great controversialists of the disbanded Society a grand chance to speak their minds, and with justifiable indignation. Innocent people rarely if ever sit down in silence after an immense mass of documentary material spread over nearly two centuries and a half has justified them. The very fact that their case was now proved to the hilt might well have sufficed for drawing this to the world's attention, especially as so many enormities were believed of them. Instead the suppression opened no mouths, set no pens to scribbling. This was because the suppression had come from the Pope, for we have often witnessed how, both before the suppression and after the restoration, there have been many Jesuits addicted to controversy. These controversies, however, have been on relatively minor points, unless a doctrine that is part of the Catholic Faith has been involved. It was completely different on this issue that was vital to the Society itself. One can only feel astounded.

We should not forget that Russia contained the rump of the Society, with a smaller fragment in Prussia. Not much could be hoped from either, for no more than a precarious protection was given in those countries to an insignificant few. Not even the most sanguine of the huge crowd of ex-Jesuits could have ventured to believe that by this means the suppressed Society could be revived. They continued of course to pray in the lonely darkness that restoration would somehow come. But it could come only through the action of a future Pope who would abrogate the brief of Clement XIV. Put in another way, they could only put their trust in God; when at last the dawn glimmered (if it ever did) they would have to start all over again — a prospect to daunt the most stouthearted.

Nevertheless a handful of members of the suppressed Society did something that helped to prepare for restoration, though their object may have been merely to huddle together in affliction. The devices thought of could not have furnished much grounds for hope; they merely indicate that hope was not quite abandoned by all, though it probably was by the majority. A couple of new religious associations were formed, in which something of the spirit of the extinct Society could be fostered. They were left unmolested only because they were small; had they grown numerous and powerful the old enemies of the Society would have been quick to accuse them of being Jesuits masquerading under a new name. Even a Pope might have considered them disobedient sons craftily trying to nullify the brief of 1773.

These small groups were guilty of nothing more than of living as secular priests in community, and with no canonical standing. They were not nearly so important in what was eventually to come as was the rump of the Society as it existed in Russia. Yet they deserve a few words, as do always those who pathetically cling to a forlorn hope.

One of these groups, which was assembled in 1797, or twenty-four years after the suppression, called themselves "The Society of the Faith of Jesus," who, perhaps because this was too close to the official title of the Jesuits, were later styled "the Fathers of the Faith." It was the idea of a not very well educated but rather remarkable man named Nicholas Paccanari, and his unofficial foundation was often known as that of the Paccanarists. The founder had never been a Jesuit but some of those who joined him were ex-Jesuits, and several of them entered the restored Society later, one of them becoming professor of philosophy at Georgetown. The avowed purpose of a few members of the little band was to work toward the revival of the Jesuits, and though in this they did not get very far, Paccanari contrived to get the approval of one of Clement XIV's successors. Even so, they faded away in 1799. Perhaps the most noteworthy thing to be recorded of them was their influence with Father Joseph Varin through whom the Religious of the Sacred Heart came into being. This congregation of nuns has proved most successful in the teaching of girls, most of them drawn from what are described as the upper classes. Varin also had much to do with the founding of a somewhat similar body, the Sisters of Notre Dame of Namur, and he was to become one of the leaders in the restoration of the Society of Jesus in France.

Another similar group was the Society of the Most Sacred Heart of Jesus. Unfortunately its founder did not have the qualities requisite for the head of such an institute, and those who joined him amalgamated with the

Paccanarists. But they attracted several very able men, one of whom — Anthony Kohlmann — subsequently became, as a Jesuit, the administrator of the diocese of New York. He is perhaps best remembered in connection with the establishment in American law courts of a principle which has never since been challenged. Summoned to give evidence obtained in the confessional from some men accused of theft, he answered: "If I did, I should render myself liable to eternal damnation," and was upheld by the presiding judge, De Witt Clinton. Another of this group who was even more remarkable was John Grassi. He affiliated with the Society in Russia and later was American superior and president of Georgetown, doing much to give prestige to that institution by his own intellectual gifts. Daniel Webster used to say that he knew no man whose conversation was more stimulating than that of this Italian Jesuit.

Though formal restoration did not come until 1814, ten years earlier Pius VII, in 1804, gave a *viva voce* permission for Jesuits outside of Russia to receive members, after which it was evident that written restoration could be considered a foregone conclusion. Even before this the signs pointed in this direction, which was a main reason for the melting away of the quasi-Jesuit groups. Though they had never been very large or very vigorous, they deserve to be remembered for what they had quietly done to pave the way for full canonical restoration when it came about.

Fourteen

Restoration

Soon after 1789 a new Europe came into being, due largely of course to the French Revolution. This, while not at all favorable to Catholicism, yet in various ways helped the Church in its work. Most of those able to escape the storm made their way to England, and though they did not convert the English, or try to do so, they did create there a more friendly attitude toward Catholicism than had prevailed since the Reformation (or perhaps it would be more accurate to say than since the usurpation of the throne by William of Orange in 1688). The courtly French abbés were discovered to be well-bred and learned gentlemen. And several religious orders were welcomed back, among which probably the chief beneficiaries were the Benedictines.

To some extent the same thing happened in the United States. When in 1790 John Carroll, himself a former Jesuit, went to England for his consecration as bishop, he hoped to secure some English priests as the recruits he so badly needed. He had already discovered that the young Americans of that day were hardly ever attracted by the priesthood, yet he somehow had to obtain a clergy, as at the outset of the American Revolution the country had just twenty-four priests, nearly all ex-Jesuits, and most of them old, infirm and discouraged. Instead of ob-

taining the British clergy, Bishop Carroll was invited by
Jacques-André Emery, the general of the Sulpicians, to
Paris, with the intention of offering some priests who
could start an American seminary. Carroll, having had
several unfortunate experiences with French clerics who
had come over during the War of Independence, did
not accept Emery's invitation, so a Sulpician Father went
to England to see him, the upshot being the founding of
St. Mary's Seminary in Baltimore. Now the work of the
Church in America came for a time to be almost entirely
under the direction of French *emigrés,* among whom one
must include Bishops Flaget of Bardstown, Bruté of Vin-
cennes, Dubois of New York, Cheverus of Boston (who
ended his days as a cardinal in France), and Maréchal
of Baltimore. Their fascinating story has no place here,
but it might be remarked that, even while preparing for
the priesthood, students from the Sulpician seminary in
Baltimore gave some help on the teaching staff of Georgetown, the first Jesuit seminary to be opened in the United
States.

Restoration did not come overnight but had been in
progress even before the Society was allowed to resume
its name in 1814, with a firmer confirmation in 1822. But
it was not easy to bring together again all the survivors
of the order that had been suppressed by Clement XIV
in 1773, and of course harder still to build up the old
organization.[1] Nobody could have foreseen that the all
but dead Society, which had had over 23,000 members at
the time of the suppression could be so astonishingly re-

---

[1] Ignatius had been obliged to ask for a couple of assistants at the
end of his life, and from this there developed the grouping of prov-
inces into "assistancies," usually along linguistic lines, a system which
still is needed, and has been further extended, for administrative purposes.

vived that today it numbers 32,501 members — nearly a fourth of whom, or 7,630, are Americans. A hundred and fifty years ago nobody could imagine such a result; even the most sanguine ex-Jesuit could at most picture a new Society of Jesus that would be but a feeble shadow of what it had been in its eighteenth-century glory.

There was indeed a nucleus with which to make a start, even leaving out of account the Jesuits in Russia and Germany and the two quasi-religious communities that sought to preserve something of the Jesuit spirit. There were here and there — especially in England, the United States, Germany, Sicily and the Low Countries — men, often banded unofficially into groups, who had established an affiliation with the Jesuits in Russia.

Even before the formal restoration, a start in this direction had been made in France, as was true of Stonyhurst in England and Georgetown in the United States. The enemies of the Society were vastly mistaken in their belief that ejections by the State followed by suppression by the Papacy had dealt a mortal blow, though it came near to being just that. The motto of the Benedictine Abbey of Monte Cassino, *Succisa virescit*, might well be that of the Jesuits, had they not already settled on one that better expresses their purpose, "To the greater glory of God," abbreviated to A.M.D.G., the first letters of this phrase in Latin.

Though the Jesuits still had powerful enemies, there had disappeared certain forces that had driven out the members of the Society and badgered the Pope into issuing the brief of suppression. The French Revolution proved to be a great factor in creating, on the one hand, a kinder feeling toward the Church, and, on the other, in ridding the Church of worldly clerics. Then Napoleon carried the Revolution in a new guise over most of Europe and even attempted to force Pope Pius VII to do his bidding, holding him as a prisoner from 1809 to 1814, until events set the Holy Father free to advance toward plans he had long cherished. And it was providential that this chance occurred, as Russia had become no longer a haven of refuge for the Jesuits, the new Czar being of an opinion vastly different from that of Catherine the Great.

Yet ancient animosities lingered on. It was not until 1829 that the Jesuits were permitted to enter Portugal once more. Then the decision was to a large extent prompted by a recognition by King Miguel of the work the Jesuits could be expected to do in the field of education. Yet though long before the suppression almost every country of Europe was made aware (if only by losing them) of the incalculable benefits that had been derived from the devotedness of the Jesuits, there were still upheavals of ungrateful and insensate rage. The favor of Portugal itself did not last for long as we shall see; the Jesuits were again driven from France by the revolution of 1830, at which time they suffered also from one of those murderous explosions that seem to be part of the Spanish temperament. In Rome itself recovery was slow until the reign of Leo XII (1823–29), and though things improved under Pope Gregory XVI, the Society did not gain the full confidence of Pius IX until after 1849.

The return of the Jesuits to Portugal has a special interest in that among the dignitaries who assembled at Lisbon to welcome the Fathers was the Marquis de Pombal, a grandson of the Society's chief enemy. He and his sister knelt before the newly arrived superior to ask forgiveness, and Donna Francesca, the sister, extracted a promise that her four sons should be received into the first college that the Jesuits reopened. Then the strangest of things happened. The Fathers found that the old Marquis had been buried with insufficient dignity in the Franciscan church at Beira. They rectified this at once, also seeing to it that a solemn requiem was sung for the repose of the cruel and corrupt man who must have been badly in need of prayers.

This, however, did not end the matter. Only five years later there was another revolution in Portugal which placed a new King, Pedro IV, on the throne, and again the Jesuits were expelled. In France, right down to living memory, the Jesuits (also religious orders in general) were tolerated or persecuted according to the complexion of the political party in power. And in Germany under Bismarck there was the *Kulturkampf*, which was not primarily an attack upon the Jesuits but upon almost all of the religious orders. Bismarck's guiding principle, as is usually the case with persecutors of the Church, was, while disavowing persecution, to bring such pressure to bear as to oblige the Church to transform itself into an instrument of secular government. In this instance the situation was saved, after a struggle that went on for about twenty years, by Ludwig Windhorst, the leader of the Centre Party, who proved himself a politician as resolute and resourceful as Bismarck himself. By Windhorst's efforts in the Reichstag, the application of the laws was gradually modified until at last Bismarck gave up a contest that he saw was going to be useless. The anti-Jesuit law, however, was never formally repealed by Bismarck and remained on the statute-book until 1917.[1]

---

[1] Many European countries have a way of allowing laws of various sorts to slip into obsolescence. Thus, when I was a Dominican novice forty years ago, it was against the law to wear a religious habit outside

A final word might be said about the restoration of the Society in England, one of the few countries in Europe in which there used always to be found a crowd to bellow "No Popery!" but in which all violent action against the Church (even against Jesuits) has long ceased. Yet in 1814 the vicars apostolic (England did not have episcopal sees until later) hesitated to recognize the Jesuits as religious, even arguing that the formal bull of restoration applied only in countries in which the civil authorities agreed to it. There was, to be sure, an exception to this, Dr. Milner not sharing the views of his colleagues. The Holy See took no definite action, as the situation in England was a delicate one, since a much more important issue — that of Catholic Emancipation — was before the country. Therefore nothing was done until 1829, the year in which Catholic Emancipation was obtained, when Pope Leo XII issued a decree that the restoration of the Jesuits applied in England as well as everywhere else.

Even after that the Jesuits now and then met with opposition by local Catholic authorities, from Cardinal Manning, for example, because he did not much like any religious orders, and had a special prejudice against the Jesuits. It was his opinion that religious orders hampered rather than promoted the work of the Church, which sounds a bit queer coming from the man who founded the Oblates of St. Charles at Bayswater.[1] But then an Englishman, of all people, must be "allowed to gang his own gait." We may safely disregard Manning's eccen-

---

of the monastery. Despite this, we took long walks in the full habit of friars on our free afternoons, well aware that we were breaking the law but that it would never be enforced.

[1] The Oblates were not, strictly speaking, an *order* but a group of secular priests living in community. But the distinction probably escapes most people.

tricity: it would be hard to find similar ideas among Catholics today. The Jesuits have over and over again showed themselves invaluable, perhaps even indispensable. It is safe to say that today, at least in English-speaking countries, the Society of Jesus is taken for granted, and that any opposition to it is all but incomprehensible.

Fifteen

Jesuit Education

IN THE EDUCATIONAL SYSTEM of Ignatius Loyola what had prevailed in the University of Paris, where he and all his first Companions had received their degrees, was accepted as the norm. The phrase *Modus Parisiensis* was always being used, as they knew of no better training, and as indeed there was none. This, however, was by no means the opinion in Italy where the first Jesuit colleges and schools were established, for Italians wished to study only what struck their fancy and to take their courses in a sequence that suited their convenience. The "elective system" therefore by no means originated in the American colleges of the end of the last century, but may almost be said to have "run amok" in sixteenth-century Italy. It was the Jesuits who really introduced the stern reform of what would be called today "required credits."

This reform was introduced by Ignatius Loyola himself (in conjunction with his friends), but it was not systematized in writing until the fifth General, Acquaviva, introduced the *Ratio Studiorum*, first in a tentative fashion in 1586, then in 1591 with some revisions after it had gone the rounds of the members of the Society for their criticism, finally in a more or less settled form in 1599. This is not to say that it is now rigidly applied by

Jesuit colleges, for some features are outmoded, but as a general summary of principles it is still well worth study.

Its aim was the education of the whole man in the best traditions of Christian humanism, and the first of its principles was that mind, will and spirit must be trained in one relation. Rules were given for the administration of the schools and their executives as well as for the individual professors of various classes. The *Ratio* provided as well for human contacts between teacher and student, and included regulations regarding the time to be spent in class and personal study and even for relaxation and exercise, since the first Jesuits were convinced of the truth of *mens sana in corpore sano.*

As for the organization of studies, in the lower classes Latin and Greek were made the basis, and if geography and history were treated merely as adjuncts of the classical texts such was the practice of other leading schools of the day, Protestant as well as Catholic. For the purpose of these classes, Grammar was divided into three sections — lower, middle and superior — which led on to instruction in Humanities and Rhetoric. For the higher education the *Ratio* prescribed courses in Theology (based on Thomas Aquinas) and Philosophy, for which the scholastic method of lecture and disputation were followed, and to these were added such scientific studies as were then in vogue — physics, astronomy, and mathematics — the authors of the document believing that these should not be undertaken until a solid literary background had been laid in the lower schools.

Already I have suggested that in the matter of the *Ratio* Ignatius may have owed something to the great humanist Vivès, whom he certainly got to know during vacations while he was himself a student at the University of Paris, and Vivès was a friend of Sir Thomas More's, who had brought him over to England and who got one of the tutors of his famously learned children to make a translation of the Spanish humanist's book into English. However the Jesuits were always ready to give the main credit to the University of Paris, because this, more than any other place, embodied the best educational methods then in vogue. But earlier in the sixteenth century Jacob Sturm, a Lutheran educational leader, had introduced something not unlike the *Ratio Studiorum* into his *gymnasium* and so claimed that the *Ratio* was derived from him. Such a claim is harmless enough, though the fact seems to be that, as Father Farrell says,[1] "the common background of the pedagogy of the sixteenth century was derived from Quintillian," with adaptations, of course, to the requirements of the age.

The educational system of the Middle Ages laid a strong emphasis on philosophy, but though it did not quite neglect science, in our sense of the term, as may be seen in St. Albert the Great (who was thought to be a necromancer because he peered into alembics), in Dante and in Leonardo da Vinci, and Francis Bacon — to give only a few examples — undoubtedly its main weakness was that it did not as a rule pay sufficient attention to anything but abstract thought. However, it need hardly be said that it was not entirely absorbed in the problem as to how many angels could dance on the point of a needle (for this was merely a gibe of one of its critics, never meant to be taken except as a joke). Similarly humanism, as in the case of the author of the *Utopia*, continued to use a racy and colloquial Latin until some later humanist (Cardinal Bembo, for instance, but also Cardinal Pole,

[1] Cf. A. P. Farrell, *The Jesuit Code of Liberal Education*, p. 357.

who passed under his influence from More's) polished and repolished their Latinity until it perished as something unfit for general use in the high Ciceronian burnish given it by the pedantically inclined. Fortunately the Jesuits, who were also humanists, were humanists of a more human stripe, so much so that it could be argued that they did more than any other group to preserve the classics from total extinction.

If in the days of the *Ratio* of 1599 more stress was placed on Latin than would be found fitting in later times, it should be remembered that in the sixteenth and seventeenth centuries Latin was the common language of the Western world, necessary for those planning to engage in law or diplomacy and indeed for all who aspired to any position in the intellectual world. Even before the suppression, the *Ratio* was revised in accordance with newer educational developments, but the classics continued to hold their place of importance, and as late as 1906 a proposal for the revision of the *Ratio* — which because of varying governmental laws for education has come to be regarded as directive rather than mandatory — reiterates its adherence to traditional methods of teaching and to the necessity of instruction in the Greek and Latin classics.

Nor for several hundreds of years were the Jesuits alone in this contention. In England, nearly down to living memory, instruction in the public schools and the universities was almost wholly in the classics. Many a man was known to have ruined what might have been a promising political career by using a false quantity in a speech in Parliament — that is, in the days when a member was expected to make a Latin quotation, however merely decorative it might be, however threadbare a tag in his

peroration. One of the few sensible remarks recorded of
George IV was made when he was known as "Prinny": "Is
the man a gentleman, does he know Greek?" If gentlemen
knew precious little beside Greek and Latin, and usually
learned them only by dint of being well flogged, they at
least acquired a good educational basis. Sir Winston
Churchill may boast that he is thankful that he was never
anything but a dullard in this department, but with all
due respect to him, one must be permitted to doubt. That
it is possible to be a very good writer of English without
having been saturated in the classics, has been proved
over and over again; how else should our literature have
produced John Bunyan or William Cobbett? But it is
hardly open to challenge that those whose education was
of the classical sort have an immense advantage, when it
comes to writing the mother tongue.

However, as we have come to the question of the inclusion of the Latin and Greek in an educational curriculum today, it must be sadly said that the second of
these has already virtually gone and that the first seems
to be on its way out. This is not the fault of the Jesuits,
but of the standardizing agencies and school boards that
have forced the Jesuits' hands. By none of these boards,
so far as I know, is Greek ever demanded and though I
believe that in many States of this country two years of
Latin is required for graduation, that time is so short that
it would be better employed upon something else. All that
happens is that the student at best gets to know the
declensions and the conjugations, which are of course an
indispensable preliminary to reading Latin, but the only
Latin he ever reads are a few simplified passages of Caesar
—which, being dry, cause him to hate Latin. He never
has much idea of the interesting technicalities connected

with it, not to mention the spirit of the language, its terseness, clarity and pungency, and he never brushes even lightly against its more interesting authors. In short, in a short space of time he completely forgets even what he has learned and never has more than an inkling that English is a "romance language" as well as one derived from Anglo-Saxon. In fact, he may hear so much praise of its "Anglo-Saxon" qualities of plainness, that he comes to think anything else artificial and affected.

This is not a plea for a return to the *Ratio Studiorum;* it contains no doubt much that is out of date, as most Jesuits themselves would admit. But this document does help to explain how the Jesuits obtained their immense reputation as teachers. It does not make the study of the classics the whole of education — far from that — but merely insists that even the most gloriously designed tower can go up only upon a foundation. And if it is true that the Jesuits are no freer than other educators of today regarding the content of their courses, they still consider themselves free as regards the spirit and method of their instruction. Leaning upon the *Ratio,* they insist that activity be demanded of the students themselves and that an attempt be made to develop in them the human faculties of intelligence, imagination, observation and reasoning power, rather than merely to supply them with an array of facts. Dissatisfaction is growing with the status of American education and with a generation upon which John Dewey has worked such havoc, and to none are its disadvantages more apparent than to the Jesuit teacher. But he is no longer alone and can afford to wait with patience, since there are signs that the tide has at last begun to turn.

A word should be said about the prominence that was

given to the drama in early Jesuit colleges, especially in France, though it can only be a word. It might be remembered that Molière was a product of Clermont. The plays were almost always written by one of the Fathers, and had edification in mind, though good acting received attention. This was not seriously handicapped — any more than it was on the Shakespearean stage — because no young women were given parts, for some young men can make up as very beautiful women, unless one is so tactless as to look at their feet. If drama clubs in modern Jesuit colleges are no better than those of similar institutions, they are assuredly no worse. The Jesuit contribution to dramatic development remains, however, one of the Society's minor glories.

At the time of the suppression in 1773 the Society of Jesus had about 750 colleges under its control, all of which were lost. But if most of that ground has never been recovered, in 1950, the latest date for which I have statistics,[1] there were 146,197 students at Jesuit colleges and universities, with 126,529 in secondary schools. There are now about 100,000 young men — and, so times have changed, young women — studying in the thirty Jesuit colleges of this country alone, with about 23,000 in its Jesuit high schools and nearly 150,000 in elementary schools taught or directed by Jesuits, and close on to 400,-000 in parish schools under their care. In Europe they conduct eleven major seminaries and thirty-two that are called minor (those which are preparatory to the seminary proper). Belonging to this last category I know of only one in the United States, that founded by Cardinal Mundelein near Chicago. It has a number of points of interest: one is that the seminary is not all under one

[1] Taken from the Supplement to the *Catholic Encyclopedia*.

roof but in a number of buildings scattered over the beautiful grounds. The Cardinal took as his architectural model the Congregational church at Old Lyme, Connecticut, a place where he used to spend his vacations when he was at Manhattan College. Another curious feature is that, while the Jesuits do all (or most of) the teaching, they have nothing whatever to do with the administration, which is in charge of diocesan priests. I have no idea how such a "separation of powers" works; for all I know to the contrary it may have been completely changed (and I would make a guess that it has been modified) since Cardinal Mundelein's death.

To say that the Jesuits opened in Campion Hall at Oxford and Southwell Hall at London University places of study for their own students, deserves recording, although it must be remembered that the Dominicans and Benedictines have done much the same thing. The crown of all is the Gregorian University in Rome, which is attended by over 2,000 ecclesiastical students, among whom there are representatives from over sixty religious orders and congregations. Only second in importance is the Pontifical Biblical Institute, with a branch in Jerusalem, and the Pontifical Oriental Institute. Even so I have enumerated only a few of the Jesuit educational undertakings.

I prescind altogether from listing the more distinguished men of the Society. The completer such a list the duller it would be, unless there was space (which there is not) to offer some comments upon the value of their achievements. Moreover, no list could be so complete but that someone of importance would not be inadvertently overlooked. An omission of this sort is sure to give somebody offense, and though people may consider me captious and cantankerous, I wish to follow St. Paul's exordium to live at peace, in so far as this lies within me, with all men.

It should however be remarked that the Jesuits, in particular those in this country, have produced a number of specialists in astronomy, meteorology and seismology. Also they have at Georgetown and St. Louis, among other places, first-rate medical schools. Their law schools are many, scattered all over the country, and Georgetown opened what is, I believe, the first School of Foreign Service this country has known. Relatively few of its students actually enter the diplomatic service, but it does give a good training to men who work in related branches. A lay professor of Georgetown also invented the method used at the Nuremberg Trials and now at the U.N. by which a speech is automatically translated into a number of different languages.

This chapter, though it is primarily concerned with education, should not overlook the many foreign missionary enterprises of the Society, especially as education itself is thought of as apostolic in purpose. But I do not have precise statistics about the matter, largely because the confusion of the war and the expulsion of all Catholic priests from Communist-dominated countries makes it almost impossible to obtain them. However, I can say that if the number of American Jesuit colleges is large, those in what have to be considered missionary lands is larger still, in the ratio of about fifty to thirty, though they are mostly small in number of students as compared with what we have. On the other hand, the primary education the Jesuits give in such countries, because of the backwardness of the people approached, is proportionately greater than is necessary in the United States with its abundance of parochial schools. We may say, therefore, that while every effort is made to reach the *intelligentsia* — and in such a country as India, by way of example, the number of Hindus and Moslems attending Jesuit schools is even larger than the number of Christians — the submerged classes are in no way neglected. The Xaverian tradition is undimmed; indeed St. Francis Xavier has for a long time been held by the Catholic Church as the patron of its missions. As Americans came relatively late into this field, they are outnumbered by the French, Belgian and Dutch, among others. But they are now climbing up rapidly, hand-over-fist, as are American missionaries as a whole, especially the Maryknoll Fathers and Sisters. Roughly, the Jesuits have 5,000 missionaries, an even larger number than they had at the time of the suppression. It might seem strange that Ireland has so far lagged behind; yet really not strange at all, when we remember what that country has done to man the parishes of neighboring England and, to a still greater extent, to reinforce the clergy of the United States.

The *Catholic Encyclopedia,* while not to be reckoned as a Jesuit undertaking, owed its inception to an American Jesuit, as is the case with the Universal Knowledge Foundation, which had to suspend its operations for lack of adequate support. One must also mention the fact that the Jesuits have produced a prodigious number of periodicals, ranging from those of a highbrow sort (such as the *Civiltá Cattolica,* the Irish *Studies,* the English *Month,* the Spanish *Razón y Fe,* the American *Thought,* and the German *Stimmen der Zeit* — I do not mention philosophical and theological learned journals — and several admirable weeklies, the best known of which in this country is *America*), down to many whose appeal is frankly popular, and which have a larger circulation, though they do not make the same mark upon Catholic intellectual life. Here, however, it is interesting to note how such a magazine as the *Messenger of the Sacred Heart* is raising its tone, a recognition of the fact that American Catholics have intellectual interests which were often lacking during immigration days. Without making any attempt to break down the figures, but grouping together about 300 Jesuit periodicals in fifty different languages, it may be said that these issue about 150,000,000 copies a year and have about 15,000,000 subscribers.[1]

As might be expected, the Jesuits are not behind other Catholics in exploiting the propaganda value of television and radio — the Pope himself now and then broadcasts messages of special importance to the whole world, and the Vatican has its own station. Though so far the Jesuits, to my knowledge, do not have a regular television program, television has been used on occasion. In the United States the chief radio program is that of WEW in St. Louis, which is carried by seven other stations, with over two thousands broadcasts a week and with an estimated ten to twelve million listeners. Other Jesuit radio stations are WWL in New Orleans and WFUV at Fordham. Much more could be done if the money were available, and would go a good way toward counteracting the

---

[1] The figure of 300 magazines belongs to the year 1915, but the Supplement to the *Catholic Encyclopedia* says the number is now well over a thousand, 26 of which had to do with general culture, 152 with higher studies and scientific investigation, 596 fostered piety, 261 promoted education and literature, and 77 dealt with the missions. These periodicals, however, vary a good deal, not only in their purpose but in their journalistic standards. In many instances the material they offer is made deliberately thin so as to accord with the taste of the readers; in still more instances it would be much better than it is if larger funds and better writers were available. The Jesuits, being realists, do the best they can with the means at their disposal, hoping that eventually a great improvement will occur, as has, in fact, often happened.

rubbish which constitutes so much of what goes out on the air waves. Eventually this may come to be, as it may be that Jesuit physicists will find a means of putting atomic power to apostolic use, but in the meanwhile it must be confessed that Jesuits (and other Catholics) are for the most part swamped by what they have to contend with.

We must never forget that the Jesuits look upon themselves as missionaries, whether it be in the field afar or at home, and that they have always been ready, even at a moment's notice, to take advantage of any means that presents itself. If in the eyes of most people they are primarily educationalists, and have been so since the days of Ignatius Loyola himself, education is with them a means to an end, the saving of souls. While a person cannot be truly educated without some knowledge of God — lacking which there can only be bewilderment in this life and utter darkness in the world to come—what so often passes for profound learning may be profound ignorance of all that really matters, and even a barrier to its reception by the mind. It is the recognition of this fact that makes the work of the Jesuits in education of such incalculable value.

Sixteen

Corporate Achievement

WHAT THE JESUIT SPIRIT IS, at least as I understand it, I hope has been gathered from the earlier chapters of this book. But many who admire the Society —
and Cardinal Newman was one of these — tell us that fine
men though the Jesuits are, they are all alike. On the face
of it, that is much too sweeping a generalization: it is impossible that there should be uniformity in characteristics
among so large a number of men.

It is true of course that, as all have started their
novitiate by making the Spiritual Exercises and have since
made a number of retreats based upon them, they bear
the stamp of the Exercises, as Ignatius Loyola intended
that they should. It is also true that the very long novitiate
through which all of them have passed has had a profound
effect, and it may be that, both because of its length and
strictness it has had even more of an effect than that derived from the novitiate of other religious orders. Because
of this there is a Jesuit "type," just as the Benedictines,
the Franciscans, the Dominicans and the rest produce a
recognizable type which is equally definite. But it simply
cannot be that training, however long and rigorous, is
able to obliterate the entire make-up of a man. In no
group is mere eccentricity encouraged for its own sake,
but every group will make allowances for the quirks of

192

human nature, on condition that they do not exceed due limit. It would be as foolish as it would be useless to aim at more.

We need not, however, rely on general considerations: those of us who have personal acquaintance with Jesuits — and it so happens that my own acquaintance with them is fairly extensive — know that, while there may be a certain amount of "family resemblance," this, as in most families, is nothing that can be called stereotyped. Human beings are never like peas all from the same pod.

So, while I write here of the Jesuit mind, I do not forget the wide dissimilarities even while stressing the type for present purposes. Sharing the classical education and intensive spiritual training which St. Ignatius obviously intended should leave a definite stamp upon every individual in his order, living in community with all that condition implies, aiming individually and collectively as their founder decreed at clothing themselves in the "vesture of Christ," it might not have been too surprising if a certain uniformity of characteristics and point of view had developed among them. Uniformity of purpose does, indeed, exist; and though implicit obedience and submission of judgment in no way preclude the use of initiative and individual intellectual capacities, on the other hand, neither does a strong instinct for, let us say, scientific research, preclude the possibility that his provincial will send a Jesuit to serve as a convent chaplain, if in his opinion that is where the priest can accomplish the greater good.

It is the usual custom, indeed, that a Jesuit throughout his life works in many varied departments of activity, so that many years of specialization in literary editorial work, for instance, are no guarantee that the next assignment may not be prison reforms, or work among the longshoremen at one of the busy ports of the world. Accepting at once in cheerful humility, the Jesuit is trained to hold himself indifferent as to what his exact job is, but to obey instantly and without question the decisions of his superiors.

The explanation is that as a rule the Jesuits have toiled without seeking any personal fame, and have preferred it so. The attainments of the group have been really stupendous, nor have all its members been able to hide their intellectual light under a bushel, try as they might. Brilliancy will, in some instances, make itself manifest, but the corruscation of stars is discountenanced.

In this connection I would like to quote from a letter written by Gerard Manley Hopkins to his life-long friend Canon Richard Watson Dixon, because it is as clear a commentary upon the Society of Jesus, in one of its aspects, as can well be found.

"Our Society," Hopkins writes, "values, as you say, and has contributed to literature, to culture; but only as a means to an end. Its history and its experience shew that literature proper, as poetry, has seldom been found to that end a very serviceable means. We had for three centuries often the flower of the youth of a country enter our body; among these how many poets, how many artists of all sorts, there must have been. But there have been very few Jesuit poets, and when they have been, I believe it would be found on examination something exceptional in their circumstances or, so to say, counterbalancing that there was in their career. For genius attracts fame, and individual fame St. Ignatius looked on as the most dangerous and dazzling of all attractions." Hopkins instances Beschi, mentioned earlier in this book as the writer of an epic poem in Tamil, as probably the best of Jesuit poets; those who wrote in English, like the Elizabethan Campion and Southwell, he ranks, of course, as good but not of major importance.

It is the same story with regard to music and painting; many Jesuits have worked well in this field without being in any way spectacular. Hopkins writes: "The persecutions, which curtailed the active ministry of Jesuits so often in some European countries, were useful in one respect: they left more Jesuits free to devote themselves to study. This may partially explain why it is that Jesuits in those countries have acquired a greater reputation than their brothers in other lands where the urgency of religious work coincided with freedom to satisfy it. Newman was right in saying that the Society has a practical and immediate work to do and goes about it in a practical way. A Jesuit may, like Carlyle, loathe schoolmastering; but if he has the spirit of his Order, he will pursue schoolmastering with enthusiasm. [This was true of Hopkins himself.] His special aptitude may even help him on uncongenial ground, which a definite and daily task may have a stabilizing influence on whatever exercise of his special talent he find the leisure for. Carlyle might have been less erratic and fantastic if he had maintained a regular and practical contact with everyday realities of a homely kind."

One may guess that Dixon, who had once taught Hopkins, did not need to be told that his former pupil was, under a veil, making a personal confession. More to the point, or at least more generally revealing, is Hopkins' comment which follows: *"Brilliancy does not suit us."*

What is to be brought out in all this is the deliberate intention of the order to present a group of men working in obedient uniformity, rather than in any individual stellar role. "The manner of living as to external things is ordinary," said St. Ignatius, and though he first said this regarding the Jesuit's avoidance of dramatic austerities, it is equally applicable to their aversion to too much singularity, with its attendant danger of intellectual pride. I have heard it put in a slightly different way: the Society aims at turning out a crack polo team, rather than a team of crack polo players. In short, the Jesuits have deliberately avoided personal celebrity, the celebrity so many of them could have won so easily, in order to cast all their talents into an impersonal pool.

One has only to review without comment the highlights of its history to demonstrate how varied have been the corporate achievements of the Jesuit order. Their positive achievements in the field of theology, canon law, history, the sciences — especially, oddly enough, seismology — and above all in their spiritual influence, have added luster to the story of the Society. In the field of education they have been a powerful factor, indeed, a trail blazer, almost from the first decade of the Society's establishment, reaching perhaps the peak of their influence in the seventeenth and eighteenth centuries in France. Their Magna Carta was the *Ratio Studiorum*, and although it has been somewhat modified by the competition of other orders and the curriculum dictated by state education associations, it is still amazingly true to its own original concept of what Catholic education should be.

In the missionary field, dating from the valiant efforts in Loyola's own lifetime of St. Francis Xavier in Asia and St. Peter Canisius in Middle Europe, we have seen the Jesuit missionaries go out all over the world, from the

Paraguay Reductions of South America to the backwoods of Canada, from the courts of China to the islands of the West Indies, with the record of the underground Church in Japan as only one example of what they have accomplished. And, to cite a strange coincidence: working together, dying together, the North American Jesuit martyrs even achieved together the crown of canonization.

In theology and canon law, we remember the work of Laynez and Salmeron and others at the Council of Trent, which defined more sharply Catholic doctrine and discipline, and that of the most notable of Jesuit theologians, the Spaniard Suarez; not to mention the philosopher-theologian Robert Bellarmine, relatively recently declared a doctor of the Church.

Then there are the enormous historical contributions of the Jesuit group known as the Bollandists, who compiled over the centuries (and are still compiling) the *Acta Sanctorum,* the history of the saints; and a work of almost similar magnitude, the *Monumenta,* which is the history of the most distinguished Jesuits, an encyclopedia of scholarship and research.

The list could be continued to the point of redundancy, with the inclusion of activities as varied as the project recently undertaken of photographing the treasures of the Vatican manuscript library, or the strides made among the labor and social injustices of our times, or the steady and undramatic work of constant retreats for religious and lay people where Jesuit guidance has contributed so much to the spiritual life of the world.

It is a matter of common observation how tenaciously a religious order adheres to the purpose for which it was primarily founded; to cite examples, the Benedictines, widely though they have broadened their work, are still

able to say, as their Rule does, that nothing is to be preferred to the *Opus Dei,* the solemn chanting in choir of
the Divine Office. The Dominicans' official title is the
Order of Preachers. The Franciscans still treasure poverty, even if unable to follow all the details of the practice of St. Francis of Assisi. But it would be difficult, if
not impossible, to say just what is the main work of the
Society of Jesus, except that it is to save souls by any
means that presents itself. All religious orders to a greater
or less extent have the same object, except the few like
the Carthusians and Trappists who are contemplatives,
and they may be no less effective in saving souls by
prayer rather than by active work. Perhaps it would not
be inaccurate to describe the Jesuits as par excellence the
great improvisors in the active apostolate.

In this there is nothing that constitutes a departure
from the Constitutions drawn up by St. Ignatius. There
is, to be sure, an enormous extension of work since the
sixteenth century, but extension is something very different from change or even modification. While the Jesuit is expected to be concerned about his personal sanctification, and is not likely to remain long in the Society
unless he is, St. Ignatius and all his successors have been
clear that they wanted the adhesion of no man who was
solely concerned about this.

One must go back here to the story of Ignatius himself: when he retired to the cave of Manresa shortly after
his conversion, he drew up the Spiritual Exercises in their
first rough form. In this he was seeking no more than the
attainment of his own perfection; only later did it dawn
on him that he had fashioned a means by which he
might make others perfect too. To a number of other
men he accordingly administered them; yet he made use

of this instrument for several years before he or his Companions thought of founding a new religious order. When they did so, they discovered that their Constitutions might be considered as the implementation of the Exercises. In that sense it perhaps might be claimed that there is no religious order in which the tradition of its sources has been more completely preserved.

One cannot think of any religious group that has had so prodigious an effect upon the world. Each of the orders, working in its own way, has magnificent achievements to its credit; but the Jesuits may be regarded as the "shock troops" of the Church, trained to strike anywhere with terrific impact. In the never-ceasing crusade of Christianity against the powers of darkness, the Jesuits advance steadily with deliberate steps, bearing with them the flame bequeathed to them by St. Ignatius Loyola—until it be reunited in the blazing warmth of the Day Spring from on high.

Bibliography

Astrain, Antonio, S.J., *Historia de la Compañía de Jesús en la Asistencia de España*, 7 vols. Madrid, 1912–25.

Barrett, Boyd, *The Jesuit Enigma*. New York, 1927.

Bertrand, J., *La Mission du Madure d'après des documents inédits*, 4 vols. Paris, 1848–54.

Böhmer, Heinrich, *Studien zur Geschichte der Gesellschaft Jesu*. Bonn, 1914. (Translated as *The Jesuits; an Historical Study*. Philadelphia, 1928.)

Bolton, Herbert E., *The Rim of Christendom*. New York, 1936.

Broderick, James, S.J., *Saint Francis Xavier (1506–1552)*. New York, 1952.

———. *The Origin of the Jesuits*. New York and London, 1940.

———. *The Economic Morals of the Jesuits*. New York and London, 1937.

———. *The Progress of the Jesuits*. New York and London, 1947.

Butler, Cuthbert, *Benedictine Monachism*. London, 1919.

Campbell, Thomas J., S.J., *The Jesuits, 1534–1921*. New York, 1921.

Catholic Encyclopedia (Supplement II) "Society of Jesus" by E. J. Burrus, unpaginated.

Charlevoix, Pierre François Xavier de, S.J., *Histoire du Paraguay, 1586–1747*, 3 vols. Paris, 1757 (English edition, 2 vols. London, 1769).

———. *Histoire de l'établissement, des progrès, et de la décadence de christianisme dans l'empire du Japan*. Lille, 1853.

Constant, Gustave, *The Reformation in England*, 2 vols. The first volume trans. by R. E. Scantlebury, the second by E. I. Watkin. London, 1934, 1941.

Coreth, Emerich, S.J., "Contemplative Action," in *Theology Digest*. Winter, 1955, pp. 37–45.

Cretineau-Joly, J.A.M., *Histoire religieuse, politique et littéraire de la Compagnie de Jésu*, 6 vols. Paris, 1844, 1851, 1856.

———. *Clément XIV et les Jésuites*. Paris, 1947.

Cronin, Vincent, *The Wise Man from the West*. New York, 1955.

Daly, James J., S.J., *The Jesuit in Focus*. Milwaukee, 1940.

Donnelly, Francis P., S.J., *Principles of Jesuit Education in Practice*. New York, 1934.

Dudon, Paul, S.J., *St. Ignatius of Loyola*. Translated by William J. Young, S.J. Milwaukee, 1949.

Farrell, A. P., S.J., *The Jesuit Code of Liberal Education*. Milwaukee, 1938.

Fülöp-Miller, René, *The Power and Secret of the Jesuits*. Translated by F. S. Flint and D. F. Tait. New York, 1930.

Garraghan, Gilbert, S.J., *The Jesuits of the Middle United States*, 4 vols. New York, 1938.

Goodier, Alban, S.J., *The Jesuits*. New York, 1930.

———. *An Introduction to the Study of Ascetical and Mystical Theology*. Milwaukee, n.d.

Graham, R. C. B. Cunninghame, *A Vanished Arcadia*. London and New York, 1901.

Guibert, Joseph de, S.J., *The Theology of the Spiritual Life*. New York, 1953.

Harney, Martin P., S.J., *The Jesuits in History*. New York, 1941.

Harvey, Robert, *Ignatius Loyola*. Milwaukee, 1936 (This, like the lives by Van Dyke and Sedgwick, is by a Protestant, but is eminently objective and fair — even if there are places into which entrance cannot be expected.)

Hughes, Philip, *A History of the Church*, 2 vols. New York, 1934–5. (Since 1954 available in abridged form as *The Popular History of the Catholic Church* in the paper-backed Image Books, issued by Doubleday.)

Hughes, Philip, *The Reformation in England,* 3 vols. New York, 1951–54.

Hughes, Thomas A., S.J., *History of the Society of Jesus in North America,* 4 vols. London, 1907–1917.

Jesuit Relations and Allied Documents. As the edition edited in 73 vols. (Cleveland, 1896–1901) by Rueben G. Thwaites would be hard to handle, it may be added that an excellent selection by Edna Kenton, first published in 1926 and reissued in 1954, would suffice for most people.

Leturia, Pedro, S.J., *Iñigo de Loyola.* Translated by Aloysius J. Owen, S.J. Syracuse, N.Y., 1949.

Loyola, Ignatius. See *Spiritual Exercises* and *Rules of the Society of Jesus.*

"Malabar Rites" in *Catholic Encyclopedia,* vol. IX.

McGucken, William J., S.J., *The Jesuits and Education.* Milwaukee, 1932.

O'Neill, J. D., "Escobar of Mendoza" in *Catholic Encyclopedia,* vol. V.

Parkman, Francis, *The Jesuits in North America in the Seventeenth Century,* 2 vols. Boston, 1910.

Pollen, John Hungerford, S.J., *Saint Ignatius of Loyola.* New York, 1922.

———. Article "Society of Jesus" in *Catholic Encyclopedia,* vol. XIV.

Ponnelle, Louis, and Border, Louis, *St. Philip Neri and the Society of his Times,* 2 vols. London, 1932.

Prescott, H. F. M., *Friar Felix at Large.* New Haven, 1950.

———. *Mary Tudor.* New York, 1953 (Reissue, with slight revisions of a former work that appeared under the name of *Spanish Tudor.* New York, 1940).

Ricci, Matthew, S.J., *China in the Seventeenth Century.* Translated from the Latin by Louis J. Gallagher, S.J. New York, 1953.

Rochemonteix, C. de, S.J., *Les Jésuits et la Nouvelle-France au XVIIIe siècle,* 2 vols. Paris, 1906.

———. *Les Jésuits et la Nouvelle-France au XVIIe siècle,* 3 vols. Paris, 1895.

Rose, Stewart (the name under which Catherine Stewart, Lady Buchan wrote), *Saint Ignatius Loyola and the Early*

Jesuits, London, 1891. I include this book here, not so much because of its scholarly merits but because it is by far the most sumptuously produced of the lives of the Saint, especially in its illustrations, and because it was the basis of Francis Thompson's more acute study.

Rules of the Society of Jesus. London, 1894 (This is not, I suspect, by any means the best edition but the only one available to me).

Sedgwick, Henry Dwight, *Ignatius Loyola.* New York, 1923.

Spiritual Exercises of St. Ignatius. Trans. from the Original Spanish, with ed. rev. Ed. by John Morris, S.J. Westminster, Maryland, 1943.

Talbot, Francis X., S.J., *Saint among Savages; The Life of Isaac Jogues.* New York, 1935.

———. *Saint among the Hurons.* New York, 1940.

———. "Society of Jesus, The," pp. 9–15 of Vol. XIII of current edition of *Encyclopedia Brittanica.*

Thompson, Francis, *Life of St. Ignatius Loyola.* London, 1909.

Van Dyke, Paul, *Ignatius Loyola.* New York, 1926.

Index

Date Due